FROM WORRY TO
WELL-BEING

HOW TO STOP WORRY
BEFORE IT STOPS YOU

GREG ERHABOR

FROM WORRY TO WELL-BEING

Copyright © Rev. Prof. G. E. Erhabor, 2010

ISBN_____

All rights reserved.
No part of this publication may be reproduced or transmitted in any form or by any means, electronic or mechanical, including photocopying, recording, or any information storage and retrieval system, without permission in writing from the author and publisher.

Concerted efforts have been made to acknowledge the author of any quotation inserted in this book. However, there may be a few omissions; especially if the authors are not known or the quotation has become part of common proverbs. The publisher however regrets any such omission.

Unless otherwise stated, all scriptures are taken from the **New International Version Bible**

Published by Spokesman Communication Ministries,
P. O. Box 1154, Ile-Ife, Osun State, Nigeria.

Printed in Nigeria.

ACKNOWLEDGEMENT

I am supremely indebted to the Almighty God for His constant presence and grace.

I am also grateful to my dear wife, Ayodele, who wholeheartedly supported me in the production of this book and daily encourages me to give full expression to the calling of God on my life. Thanks for being a great partner.

CONTENTS

Acknowledgement		**III**
Contents		**V**
Introduction	- Why another book on worry?	**VII**
Chapter One	- Worry: What is it?	1
Chapter Two	- Biblical perspective of worry	11
Chapter Three	- Why do men worry?	31
Chapter Four	- Consequences of worry	55
Chapter Five	- How to handle worry	79
Chapter Six	- Trust: the victory over worry	133
Chapter Seven	- Taking captive of your thoughts and imaginations	149
Chapter Eight	- When there seems to be a delay	171
Chapter Nine	- How great men handled their worry	191
Chapter Ten	- You must quit worrying now	213
Epilogue		**217**

INTRODUCTION

WHY ANOTHER BOOK ON WORRY?

It has been said that many people will die, not from the problems they face but from the habit of continuous worry and anxiety about the problems they go through. Worry has been described as the number one public enemy of mankind. As a physician of over three decades, I have come to the conclusion that worry and anxiety are at the root of many diseases and worry has the capacity of aggravating and turning a seemingly harmless condition into a more serious disease.

This book came as a result of my experience with numerous people as a physician, a pastor, a teacher and a counselor. I have experienced the effect of worry in my life and I have also seen it devastate family members and friends. In this book, I have attempted to look at the root cause of worry and suggest ways by which we can win over worry and live a life of buoyancy and freedom. The book is not a one-time solution to all our worries but it will help us in our quest to conquer this evil habit.

Worry is a great sin because it destroys our faith in God and without faith it is impossible to please Him. Regardless of the nature of your worry or how long you have indulged this habit, you can take a definite step to free yourself from this bondage. Peter puts it simply, "Casting all your care upon him; for He cares for you" (1Peter 5:7). That is the key. You either allow your cares to destroy you or you hand it over to God. Be determined to stop worry before it stops you!

CHAPTER ONE

WORRY: WHAT IS IT?

> "And Jesus said to his disciples, therefore I tell you do not be anxious and troubled (with cares) about your life, as to what you will (have to) eat: or about your body as to what you will have to wear ...And which of you by being overly anxious and troubled with cares can add a cubit to his stature or a moment [unit] of time to his age [the length of his life]? If then you are not able to do such a little thing as that why are you anxious and troubled with cares about the rest?"
>
> **Luke 12:23, 25-26 Amplified Version**

Worry has continued to be one of the major problems facing and threatening the existence of man. The search for an escape in the form of civilization has done little, if any, in solving this problem. In fact, the geometric increase in urbanization has complicated and compounded our worries. The promise of technology has failed to produce positive results in the mental state of the populace and attempts by world bodies to bring peace to the nations have not been completely successful. Efforts at creating diversions have provided only temporary comforts. At the end of a false sense of ecstasy and pleasure, many simply fall back into the deep and scary pit of anxiety.

Statistics have revealed the appalling rate at which men elect to end their lives. A data from the World Health Organization showed that every year, almost one million people die from suicide; a "global" death rate of 16 per 100,000, or one death every 40 seconds. In the last 45 years, suicide rates have increased by 60% worldwide. On the average in the United States of America, one person (male or female) takes his own life every 16 minutes. Suicide is the 11th ranking cause of death for all Americans and the third leading cause of death for young people aged 15-24 year olds (National Institute of Mental Health). You might ask: why do people choose suicide? Why do they wish to end their lives? Many reasons including social isolation, divorce, unemployment, loss of loved ones, mental illness, depression and feelings of hopelessness have been given. But at the root of all these lie the basic reason: worry! Studies in the US have shown that up to one fifth of Americans worry at such an alarming rate as to require medical attention (National Institute of Mental Health).

Worry has resulted in divorce in many homes and has made people lose hope in the future. It has driven men to the pit of depression and led them along the thorny path of schizophrenia. With over three decades of experience in medical practice, I have discovered that worry is at the root of many diseases. The evil effects of this worldwide epidemic are innumerable. Considering the immense implications of worrying, I believe we need to have an in-depth knowledge of what it is and how to handle it.

> Someone who is worried is under pressure about the situation; and the problem is no more the situation, the problem is his worry.

WHAT IS WORRY?

Worry is the greatest expression of doubt in God. It is a destructive mental habit, which has been acquired over time and with prolonged accumulation becomes hard to break. Worry complicates issues and gets things muddled

> **Worry is the greatest expression of doubt in God.**

up. The scripture above emphasizes '*do not be anxious and troubled.*' This is exactly what worry is: being unduly troubled. Jesus was not just talking about our having cares about what we shall eat or how hard to work in our personal lives, but he is also stressing that kind of care that drains our energy and diverts our focus.

To worry is to "feel uneasy or anxious, fretting, tormenting oneself with or suffering from disturbing thoughts." Worry robs you of the inner strength required to face the storms of life. It removes insight and makes convictions shallow and changeable. Worry is a condition that must be avoided. It is the cause of most damage and grief around us. The destructive nature of worry is evidenced by its derivation from an Anglo-Saxon word which means 'to choke.' The way you choke when someone tightens his fingers around your throat dramatizes the impact of worry on your spiritual and physical life. Worry cuts the supply of your spiritual oxygen and deprives your spirit, soul and body of important nutrients necessary for development.

The Webster's Third New International Dictionary defines worry as *'to feel or experience concern, disquietude or anxiety and to fret.'* It defines fret as *'a rancorous eating or gnawing at or a continuing vexing that leaves one no peace'* and went further to define anxiety as *"a mental distress or agitation resulting from concern usually for something impending or anticipated."* The eye-opening fact about these definitions is that worry is a mental distress, which leaves one with no peace. Unfortunately, it is usually for something anticipated. Ninety percent of what we worry about is non-existent: things we feel might happen.

> Worry cuts the supply of your spiritual oxygen and deprives your spirit, soul and body of important nutrients necessary for development.

Through research, it has been estimated that we perform a great deal of unnecessary worry. Earl Nightingale, in *Lead the Field,* documented the result of a study done on the things we worry about. He said the things for which we worry can be broken down as follows: Things which never happen - 40 percent, things past which can't be changed or corrected - 30 percent, needless worry about our health - 12 percent, petty miscellaneous worries - 10 percent, real and legitimate worries - 8 percent. Many people have ended up in mental homes, courtesy worry. It has resulted into many deaths and someone commenting on this dreadful scourge said, 'It is not work that kills but worry.'

The Message Bible translates **Matthew 6:25-34** explicitly:

> "If you decide for God, living a life of God-worship, it follows that you don't fuss about what's on the table at mealtimes or whether the clothes in your closet are in fashion. There is far more to your life than the food you put in your stomach, more to your outer appearance than the clothes you hang on your body. Look at the birds, free and unfettered, not tied down to a job description, careless in the care of God. And you count far more to him than birds. "Has anyone by fussing in front of the mirror ever gotten taller by so much as an inch? All this time and money wasted on fashion--do you think it makes that much difference?
>
> Instead of looking at the fashions, walk out into the fields and look at the wildflowers. They never primp or shop, but have you ever seen

color and design quite like it? The ten best-dressed men and women in the country look shabby alongside them. If God gives such attention to the appearance of wildflowers-- most of which are never even seen--don't you think he'll attend to you, take pride in you, do his best for you? What I'm trying to do here is to get you to relax, to not be so preoccupied with getting, so you can respond to God's giving. People who don't know God and the way he works fuss over these things, but you know both God and how he works. Steep your life in God-reality, God-initiative, God-provisions. Don't worry about missing out. You'll find all your everyday human concerns will be met. Give your entire attention to what God is doing right now, and don't get worked up about what may or may not happen tomorrow. God will help you deal with whatever hard things come up when the time comes."

At the time Jesus uttered this statement, the world was less complicated. They did not have cars or planes; the luxuries of comforters and internal heating system were not at their disposal. One would have thought that with the advent of fast cars, quick meals and easy accessibility to life's comforts, our generation would be free of worry.

However, in spite of our sophistication and possessions, things are not better. People are still worried and disturbed; they are still unhappy. I think it brings to bear the fact that external factors are not key determinants of internal peace.

Many of the problems we have, has little or nothing to do with the situations we face but with the habit and culture of worry. Somebody may ask: is it possible not to worry? I believe it is possible. When you look at the life of Jesus, you will discover he enjoyed a peaceful and worry-free life. There were times it seemed He was troubled but He was able to harness the power of God to handle those situations. In the Garden of Gethsemane, his heart was deeply troubled and he cried to God three times to remove his cup of suffering. But He submitted to the will of God and he was strengthened for the task ahead.

There is a difference between worry, which gets you stressed by the situation, and concern, which stimulates you to do something about your situation. Someone who is worried is under pressure about the situation; and the problem is no more the situation, the problem is his worry. But somebody who is concerned looks at the situation and uses it as a stimulus to find the solutions.

Concern leads to problem-solving while worry leads to a pressure of the mind. Here Jesus is concerned about us making worry a habit, making it a part of our culture or part of our being. You become very good at whatsoever you do very often. Those who worry and keep on worrying become professionals in worrying. They eventually lose control of their lives and subject their destiny to the whims of fate.

> Concern leads to problem-solving while worry leads to a pressure of the mind.

There is an ancient folktale of how the messenger of death was sent to kill a thousand people in a country. Before he set out, rumours went about the nation that death was coming. About a thousand people collapsed as a result of the rumour. As 'death' approached, people started running helter-skelter and 500 people died from the ensuing stampede. When 'death' finally arrived, he killed one thousand people. On reporting back, he was asked why he had killed more than planned, he quickly replied that he only fulfilled his assignment; the rest were killed by fear, worry and anxiety. This story goes to illustrate the fact that more people die from worry than death itself. We should worry more about our worries for they are actually destroying the life in us.

Worry puts our minds in a state of turmoil and chaos. The mental faculty is disorganised and disoriented. Plans and decisions cannot be made and the ones made cannot be effectively carried out. Worry divides the mind into many disjointed pieces. It creates an arena where good and bad thoughts are jumbled up to produce an unwelcoming disarray. In reflection, Robert Albert Bloch said, "Worry is a small trickle of fear that meanders through the mind until it cuts a channel into which all other thoughts are drained."

CHAPTER TWO

BIBLICAL PERSPECTIVE OF WORRY

> We can easily manage if we will only take, each day, the burden appointed to it. But the load will be too heavy for us if we carry yesterday's burden over again today, and then add the burden of the morrow before we are required to bear it.
>
> **John Newton**

William Barclay, the great Scottish theologian analyzed the meaning of the word 'worry' in his book *New Testament Words*. Worry, he said, is derived from the Greek Word *'merimnan,'* which means 'to take thought for or to be anxious about.' The noun *'merimna'* means care, thought or anxiety. It is the word that is used for the cares of this world, which choke the life out of the good seed of the word of God. The verb *merimnan* has its most important use in the Sermon on the Mount. Jesus says in **Matthew 6:25**,

> "**Therefore I tell you, stop being perpetually uneasy (anxious and worried) about your life, what you shall eat or what you shall drink; or about your body, what you shall put on. Is not life greater (in quality) than food and the body (far above and more excellent) than clothing?**" **(AMP)**

Wycliffe, a translator of the Bible translated this verse as, "Be not busy for your life." Tyndale, Crammer and the Geneva Bible translate it as, "Be not careful of your life" in which the translation 'careful' has its literal meaning as 'full of care.' The Revised Standard version puts it this way: "Be not anxious for your life." Moffatt translation says, "Do not trouble about what you are to eat and drink in life" while Weymouth has this: "I charge you not to be over anxious about your lives." The New Testament in Plain English translates it as, "Worry no more about your life" and Schofield in the Authentic New Testament has, "Do not vex yourselves about what you are to eat or drink." The New Living Translation says, "So I tell you, don't worry about everyday life."

Worry is a habit that affects most of us. Bill Sherill, author and writer, wrote, "We are such a worrying people! Some of us certainly more than others! I can remember so clearly how my mother seemed to have perfected the art. I would receive a letter while away at school warning me to stay away from the water for a time because she had a bad dream. Of course it was a little difficult for me to oblige since one of my jobs was to care for the college pool as well as act as a water safety instructor. Mother was a good God-fearing woman, but she had a little trouble with "be not anxious." Mother was not in a class by herself. Many today continue to find it difficult to trust the future to God."

> Many today continue to find it difficult to trust the future to God.

Jesus knew that when we worry we lose our trust in God. He understood that worry robs us of faith, peace and trust in our heavenly Father; so He instructed against it. Bishop Fulton J. Sheen said, 'Worry is a form of atheism, for it betrays a lack of faith and trust in God.' Worry makes us to anticipate troubles, which seldom come to those who believe in God. And this is a crime against God, man, nature and better judgement.

John R. Rice commented, "Worry is putting question marks where God has put periods." The promises of the Bible are usually questioned by the worrier's mind. When the Bible declares, *"For with God nothing will be impossible"* **(Luke 1:37)**, an anxious man asks, 'Is that really true?' In worrying, we often see the negative side of issues; the obstacles in the situation. We overlook the opportunities thus setting negativism in motion and spreading it everywhere we go. Worry is contagious. A man, who worries, spreads it to his wife and children. An employer who worries will soon have all the workers in the company worrying. Except someone decides to break out, a generation of worriers soon develop. Worry diminishes our productive capabilities. Many students fail, not because they are not brilliant but because of anxiety. The time, which should be invested in studying, is being spent worrying.

Whatsoever we might be going through in life, worry is not the solution. It compounds the problems, prevents us from doing the right things and from taking the right steps. Worry empties today of its strength. *'Do not worry'* is a commandment which if obeyed brings peace to the soul, health to the body and growth to the spirit. It gets us focused on our divine purpose. When we care about the things of this world, we forget the heavenly goal; in being anxious about our bodily needs, our minds are closed to the majesty of the most High God, who has all things in His power. Worry reduces our faith in God. In fact, worry is an antithesis of the Christian faith.

> 'Do not worry' is a commandment which if obeyed brings peace to the soul, health to the body and growth to the spirit.

Jesus in His teachings opened our eyes to God's provisions. Paul, in his letter to the Philippians, wrote,

> **"And my God will meet all your needs according to his glorious riches in Christ Jesus"** **(Philippians 4:19).**

God is able to supply all our needs. However, in anxiety, we fail to acknowledge God as our source of supply and our place of refuge. We simply drift away, looking for ways and means of solving our problems and caring for ourselves. **Psalm 24:1** says,

> "The earth is the Lord's and everything in it, the world and all who live in it."

If God owns everything in the world, then we just need to apply for fresh supplies every day. We have to stop worrying and tune in to the owner of all things. 'Give us this day our daily bread' is a prayer that is sufficient for the day. God daily loads us with blessings. He is a 'daily' God; a 'Now' God.

Worry **prevents us from seeing the need for thanksgiving** in everything. Whenever Jesus wanted to do a miracle, he first gave thanks to God. It is quite amazing the rate at which he multiplied things simply by giving thanks! When we worry, we forget all that the Father has done for us thereby shutting the door to more blessings and provisions by the Lord. God doesn't want us to worry about anything but rather to give thanks. A person that gives thanks encourages more giving. Paul says in **1 Thessalonians 5:18**,

> "Give thanks in all circumstances, for this is God's will for you in Christ Jesus."

This is God's will and as children of God we have to do His will. **Philippians 4:6-7** says,

> "Do not be anxious about anything, but in everything, by prayer and petition, with thanksgiving, present your requests to God. And the peace of God, which transcends all understanding, will guard your hearts and your minds in Christ Jesus."

This peace of God will continue to elude us as long as we practice anxiety. We need to drop all our worries to be beneficiaries of God's peace. **1 Peter 5:7** says,

> "Cast all your anxiety on him because he cares for you."

God cares for us and He has the strength required to carry all our problems. We do not have to burden our frail mortal bodies with them for they will weigh us down both spiritually and physically. **Psalm 37:1** begins, "Do not fret..." and verse 8 repeats the advice, "Do not fret"

(NKJV). The Good News Bible says, "Don't be worried." Why? Because worrying causes harm. It does damage to our minds and health and creates more problems. Besides, it doesn't change the situation. *"And who of you by worrying and being anxious can add one unit of measure (cubit) to his stature or to the span of his life?"* **(Matthew 6:27).** None of us can do this! Yet many people worry because of the shape of their bodies, the size of their nose or the colour of their fingernails.

Worry serves as **a form of diversion** from the things of God. When we worry, we stop studying the Word of God and start looking for solutions where they do not exist. Worry is an obstacle to a successful prayer life. He who worries does not have a full capability to seek God in prayer and he who prays does not worry. The two are opposite and we have all been given the opportunity to choose one. Anxiety chokes the Word of God in our lives. It opposes the spirit of God in us and contradicts God's promises.

The cares of life cause us to doubt the testimonies of God, prevents the seed of the Word from germinating in our lives and hinders the good results which come from obeying God's commandments from materializing.

Luke 8:14 says,

> "And as for what fell among the thorns, these are (the people) who hear but as they go on their way, they are choked and suffocated with the anxieties and cares and riches and pleasures of life, and their fruit does not ripen (come to maturity and perfection)."

The cares of life do not only choke the Word of God in our lives, they also prevent us from bearing the fruits of the Spirit. The gospel according to **Matthew 13:22** says,

> **"As for what was sown among thorns, this is he who hears the Word but the cares of the world and the pleasure and delight and glamour and deceitfulness of riches choke and suffocate the Word and it yields no fruit."**

God wants us to bear fruits. He wants us to be productive. In order to achieve this, we must stop worrying about the future. We must understand that our lives are secure in Christ Jesus. We must learn to tackle today's problems and let tomorrow cater for itself. Worry is the interest we pay on tomorrow's troubles.

CHAPTER THREE

WHY DO MEN WORRY?

> "But take heed to yourselves and be on your guard, lest your hearts be overburdened and depressed [weighed down] with the giddiness and headache and nausea of self indulgence, drunkenness and worldly worries and cares pertaining to [the business of] this life and [lest] that day come upon you suddenly like a trap or a noose."
>
> **Luke 21:34 AMP**

Through the ages, the reasons and causes of man's worries have gradually changed. Perhaps the stone-age man would have worried about being attacked by a wild animal while the twenty first century man will be worrying about the next model of i-phone, but one peculiar need is common to all men through these years: the need for food, clothing and shelter. Besides these, other reasons for worry abound. They range from the threat of global warming to the collapse of the stock market, from the late coming of the tropical rains to the endemic diseases that plague man's environment. These reasons span the entirety of man's existence from birth till death. It applies to his activities from dawn till dusk. In the next few paragraphs, we will be examining the major causes of worry in man.

UNHEALTHY COMPARISON - A COMPETITIVE SPIRIT

Can you imagine? Teju already has a good job, a luxurious car and a beautiful wife. After all I was more brilliant than him at school. It seems things are not just working for me. Oh God, what will I do? I am 30 years, all my sisters and brothers got married before the age of 27 years; there must be something wrong with me. My father had his first house before he was 40 years, now I am 50 but have not got my own house. All my colleagues that I started with have really gone far; what have I been doing?'

Statements like these are not uncommon among us,

Christians and non-Christians alike. Several people have fallen victim of the 'comparison syndrome.' Many are worrying themselves to death because of another man's successes. We forget that the pathway for each of us is different. We cannot all be the same. We cannot be equal in our levels of wealth, understanding and knowledge. The Bible says in **2nd Corinthians 10:12**,

> **"...However when they measure themselves with themselves and compare themselves with one another, they are without understanding and behave unwisely."**

One of the most important reasons we worry is that we measure ourselves with other people. The Bible says by measuring or comparing ourselves with others we become fools. Look at anybody you have compared yourself with, or anyone you have been jealous of and pause a little while. If God decides to exchange everything he has with yours, would you like it? Would you accept his poor health along with the wealth? Somebody once said that if one knows the troubles and worries that millionaires go through, no one would ever want to become one.

We cannot afford to compare because **there are no**

universal rules for measurement. Someone may be wealthy in gold yet poor in joy. Another may be gorgeous in appearance yet an intellectual dwarf. Another may have several opportunities open to him in one particular area and yet in another area he may be a complete novice. There are no universal rules to measure people. If your worry is based on the fact that someone is ahead of you then you are not wise. There are aspects of your life in which you are also ahead. Stop using another person's yardstick for your life. God is not going to look at anyone in order to measure your situation and He will not use another's blueprint to pattern your life.

Besides, we do not need to compare because **every one of us is unique** in his way. Each individual is a unique creation of God. Two individuals cannot exactly be alike. Even identical twins still have differences. We all have different approaches to life and different ideas about it. David declared:

> "I will praise You, for I am fearfully and wonderfully made; marvellous are your works, and that my soul knows very well." (Psalm 139:14 NKJV)

Paul told the Ephesians,

> "**Yet to each of us <u>individually</u> grace was given, measured out with the munificence of Christ**" **(Ephesians 4:7 Weymouth New Testament).**

Unhealthy comparison is a disease that we must resist with the promises of God's Word. It creates unwholesome competitiveness and generates all kinds of stress. Many parents have created friction in their homes because of the way they compare their children and undermine the potentials of one child because of the other. One child may be good in analysis of complex equations and at storing facts. He may turn out to be very brilliant in school and score high grades, whereas, the other child may have unusual creative abilities. Such a child may not score high grades in school but he will be a great person, if encouraged. Exposing such child to criticism will make him feel inferior to his sibling and turn him to a worrier.

> God will give us success in His time.

God will give us success in His time. Your situation, your physical appearance, how much money you have, your upbringing, your race or the culture does not matter. God can give you success in your time. Why? Because He is a God of variety. That is evident even from nature. He does things in a unique manner. God takes ordinary things and makes extraordinary models out of it. There are no universal measurements but in your own unique style, God will lead you. I met a lady sometime ago who said her greatest regret was having studied medicine. I asked her why and she said she spent twelve years in medical school; what more, all her younger sisters have gotten married and had kids. They have built houses and settled in their homes while she was spending years studying for a degree. Well, I advised her to learn to give thanks. I am very sure if you meet those sisters of hers, they will introduce themselves in relation to her. They might probably say I am the sister of Dr. Jane. They will be proud to have a sister who is a doctor whereas she was unhappy that she was not like her sisters.

If only you can sit with yourself and find exactly what God has called you to do, you will arrive at your destination. Oswald Chambers, Scottish minister and author of widely-read devotional *My Utmost for His Highest* said, "All worry is caused by calculating without

> When you look at other peoples' lives and scheme based on their achievements, you end up being a mediocre.

God." When you look at other peoples' lives and scheme based on their achievements, you end up being a mediocre. But that is not the way God wants it. Albert Einstein, one of the most influential scientists of all time, said, "He who marches in rank and file has already earned my contempt; he has been given a large brain by mistake, since for him the spinal cord will suffice." Albert was saying that we cannot expect to pattern our lives according to that of others and expect to be extraordinary. What works for one person might not necessarily work for others.

There was a time it was said that the secret of church growth is evangelism from house to house. People started going from house to house. Later some people said the secret is in house groups; many churches changed their strategy and started having house groups. Another group came up to say the secret is in crusades; people started organizing all kinds of crusades from place to place. However, I noticed that most churches who imitated those formulas never grew. Somewhere inside your spirit is your winning formula; if only you can sit you down before God and find it out.

John F. Kennedy, the thirty-fifth American President said, "Conformity is the enemy of thought and the jailer of freedom." By comparing ourselves, we are missing out on our uniqueness. I have come to see people that the world thought will never amount to anything become great people. You are a bundle of talents; use your potentials. You break the worry habit when you begin to question the status quo; when you begin to question the way things are going.

> Somewhere inside your spirit is your winning formula; if only you can sit down before God and find it out.

Moreover, when we compare ourselves with people, we forget that **there is something underneath** everything we are seeing. You see a very rich man who has several houses and wish you were like him; just take a little look at the source of his wealth. The man may be on several loans; in fact, he may owe the bank so much money that he finds it difficult to sleep. What is underneath? There was a time I went somewhere to preach and I saw this wonderful couple. They were the perfect picture of an ideal couple. The man treated his wife with courtesy and everything seemed to be working well for them. Later I told the man, 'I'm so impressed by your marriage, I wish I could emulate you.' He said, 'That is okay but this woman you are seeing is my third wife, the first and second are somewhere else.' Behind what you are admiring is something. No one is complete in himself; our 'completeness' is found only in God. The Psalmist said,

> "For I was jealous of the proud, when I saw the peace of the wicked... When I thought deeply in order to understand this, it was painful for me, until I went into the sanctuary of God; then I understood their end. Surely You set them in slippery places; You cast them down into ruin" (Psalms 73:3, 16-18).

God made him to understand the end.

Life is a process. Don't begin to judge your life by where you are now. You don't know the end of your life yet. You don't know what God has in His plan for you. Understand that the purpose of life is much more than the peripheral and the material things

No one is complete in himself; our 'completeness' is found only in God.

that choke us. Don't form the habit of worry. Because if you do, the Bible says you are sinning. And the more you sin, the more you get worried. Are you taking briefs from another person's script? Are you looking at another player and trying to imitate his manoeuvers? Are you dancing to another person's rhythm? God will make you succeed in your own time.

You must come to the realization that your gifts and potentials are yours and you have to maximize them to get to your place in destiny. Another man's gifts are his and no matter how hard you try to be like him, you can only succeed in being an imitation.

COVETOUSNESS

Covetousness is a sin that incurs worry and leads to destruction. It is a spirit that has nothing to do with how much you have but the desire to have more. A covetous man is never satisfied. If he has a car he will desire another man's car. If he sees someone else's clothes, he will start thinking of buying it. He compares himself with another person and begins to get anxious.

King Ahab in the Bible was a typical example of a person whose greed led to anxiety and eventual destruction. 1 King 21:1-4 records,

"Sometime later, there was an incident involving a vineyard belonging to Naboth the Jezreelite. The vineyard was in Jezreel, close to the palace of Ahab king of Samaria. Ahab said to Naboth, let me have your vineyard to use for a vegetable garden since it is close to my palace. In exchange, I will give you a better vineyard or if you prefer, I will pay you whatever its worth." But Naboth replied, "The Lord forbid that I should give you the inheritance of my fathers. So Ahab went home sullen and angry because Naboth the Jezreelite had said, I will not give you the inheritance of my fathers." He lay on his bed sulking and refused to eat." (NIV)

In spite of King Ahab's wealth, he still desired to have another person's property. Many people are not content with what they have. They crave for money, wealth and material possessions. Covetous people desire to be rich and would go to any length to be wealthy. **1 Timothy 6:10** says,

> "For the love of money is a root of all evils, it is through this craving that some have been led astray and have wandered from the faith and pierced themselves through with many acute [mental] pangs!" (AMP)

Worrying about possessions causes mental distress. It destabilizes the system and makes the person lose his self-worth. **Habakkuk 2:15** says,

> "Moreover, wine and wealth are treacherous; the proud man (the Chaldean invader) is restless and cannot stay at home. His appetite is large like that of Sheol and (his greed) is like death and cannot be satisfied he gathers to himself all nations and collects all people as if he owned them."

Whosoever loves money would never have enough. Anyone who has a passionate desire for wealth cannot be easily satisfied. **Ecclesiastes 4:8** says,

> "There is one alone-no one with him; he neither has child nor brother. Yet there is no end to all his labour, neither is his eye satisfied with

riches neither does he ask, for whom do I labour nor deprive myself of good? ..."

The spirit of covetousness pushes a man to desire more and worry more. **Ecclesiastes 1:8** says,

> "All things are weary with toil and all words are feeble; a man cannot utter it. The eye is not satisfied with seeing nor the ear filled with hearing."

Many people are miserable simply because they are covetous. Covetousness entangles a man and pushes him to acquire what he should not.

The opposite of covetousness is contentment. Contentment has nothing to do with how much money you have in your account. It has nothing to do with what you earn. Contentment is a state of spiritual equilibrium, that 'if I'm in need, I bless God, for my God shall supply the deficit and when I'm in surplus, my God shall help me distribute the surplus.' In whatsoever situation I am in, I can maintain spiritual and mental equilibrium; I can be calm within, knowing that

> *Contentment is a state of spiritual equilibrium.*

He will never leave me desolate or forsake me. As Paul wrote,

> "Not that I speak in regard to need; for I have learned in whatever state I am, to be content" (Philippians 4:11 NKJV).

If we will stop worrying, we must come to that point of contentment. We must bless God for what He is doing in our lives. Somebody asks, 'Does contentment mean we should be complacent?' No! Contentment is not complacency. It means you are aspiring to the next level but while you are at it, you can rejoice in the Lord your Maker in this level. You can say, 'it is well with my soul.' Reflect on the fact that if God has led you this far, the rest of the journey will be easy for Him to handle. Rest your soul and trust God.

ABSENCE OF THE CORE QUESTIONS OF LIFE

Men get worried when they don't ask the core questions of life: *Why all these? Where am I going? What is the essence of life? Is this thing necessary? Can't I do without this? What is the real important issue of life? Why am I here?*

Christ's teachings opens our eyes to the fact that food, clothing and shelter may be essential but they are not the essence of life. Although they are good, they are not the most important things. Life is more than all the things we crave for. *"Is not life greater than all these things"* **(Matthew 6:25).** Core questions about life enable us to see existence in a deeper perspective. They propel us to do the things that are of value and last long. Core questions elevate us from the ordinary to the level of the supernatural. They make us see life from God's viewpoint. The church of Christ was not established for food and drinks, neither was it instituted to provide husbands and wives; it was established to propagate the gospel of Christ and expand the kingdom of God. This is the High calling of God by Christ Jesus.

In asking and finding answers to life's questions, we are gradually weaned from a parochial outlook to understanding the purpose of God. When we ask these questions, we will not only hold our lives in high regard, but we will also focus on fulfilling the purpose of God for our lives. The Preacher, after deep introspection, said,

> "Let us hear the conclusion of the whole matter. Fear God, and keep His commandments. For this is the whole duty of man" (Ecclesiastes 12:13 NKJV).

Prophet Jeremiah said,

> "Thus says the LORD: "Let not the wise man glory in his wisdom, Let not the mighty man glory in his might, Nor let the rich man glory in his riches; But let him who glories glory in this, That he understands and knows Me, That I am the LORD, exercising lovingkindness, judgment, and righteousness in the earth. For in these I delight," says the LORD" (Jeremiah 9:23-24 NKJV).

When we understand the basis of our existence, we would overlook our few discomforts and concentrate on making life better for our fellow men; we would pursue the kingdom of God. The pursuit of God's kingdom attracts other favours and ensures the provision of our necessities.

> "But seek first the kingdom of God and His righteousness; and all these things shall be added to you" (Mathew 6:33).

The core questions of life help us to find the compass of life. When men lose their compass, they are turned around by every wind of doctrine, and are gullible to different kinds of beliefs. We must learn to sift information in order to separate the good from the bad. Otherwise we will bring problems on ourselves. Quite a number of people are in hot pursuit of ephemeral things like cars, houses, clothes and other material things. Many are struggling to acquire degrees because every other person is doing that, but the big question is: Do these things give joy? Are these things supposed to be the end of the means or means to an end?

Many believe that making money and being wealthy defines a fulfilled life. Yet, many rich men are sorrowful and full of worries. They would gladly give up everything just to have happiness and peace of mind. Joy does not depend on the abundance of your possessions. **Luke 12:15** reads, *"...for one's life does not consist in the abundance of the things he possesses."* The compass of life is not making money, it is finding God. And when people miss out on that divine direction, their lives would be filled up with worry.

Have you stopped to think about all that God has given you since you came into existence? Do you know that God has created you a more valuable entity than all the little things you worry about? Have you given Christ a place in your life? There was once a rich man who was glorious in his wealth. He said to his soul,

> "Soul you have many good things laid up, (enough) for many years. Take your ease; eat drink, and enjoy yourself merrily. But God knocked at his door, 'You fool, this very night they will demand your soul of you ...." (Luke 12:19-20).

Verse 21 says,

> "So it is with the one who continues to lay up and hoard possessions for himself and is not rich (in his relation) to God (this is how he fares)."

God made that man recognize that it is not wealth that determines one's life, it is God who gives a meaning to life. He is the one who puts value to it. He is the compass that steers the boat of life in the right direction. God is the only one who can make that much-needed difference in one's life.

A life that recognizes the core issues is elevated above the problems and worries of a restless world and dwells in the tranquillity of a continual communion with God. It is immune to the storms that toss the ship of life. It is a peaceful existence.

COMPLICATIONS OF LIFE

Worry results when our lives get complicated. The twentieth century has brought sophistication coupled with its attendant problems. New things make us think the old is bad and unnecessary. We have become very civilised and refined. Various kinds of drinks, foods and means of transportation abound to attend to our needs and supposedly make us comfortable. However, most of these things bring encumbrances into our lives. By the time you buy electronic equipment, it is already out of date. In fact, the speed with which products are being released into the market creates urgency in the average materialistic person to acquire more property. This generates a lot of worries in a world where having the latest thing is in vogue. We are burdened with many problems in the name of technological advancement. Our houses are filled up with junks we seldom use, and our minds are filled with information we rarely need.

Samuel Johnson said, "The desires of man increase with his acquisitions; every step which he advances brings something within his view, which he did not see before and which as soon as he sees it, he begins to want. Where necessity ends, curiosity begins; and no sooner are we supplied with everything that nature can demand, than we sit down to contrive artificial appetites." The invention of new things to satisfy our appetites increased our worries. It makes life complex and generates problems that drain the energy that sustains our existence.

INNER CONFLICT- YOUR THOUGHT LIFE

The mind is an arena of great conflict between good and evil thoughts. He is a great man, who is able to control and constructively channel his thoughts. Conflicting thoughts and imaginations give our souls internal unrest. Many people insinuate things that are not there; they try

> He is a great man, who is able to control and constructively channel his thoughts.

to read other people's mind and interpret their actions based on this, and this leads to a lot of worries. It is true that a lot of negative thoughts pass through our minds daily.

Genesis 6:5 says,

> "And GOD saw that the wickedness of man was great in the earth, and that every imagination of the thoughts of his heart was only evil continually."

Jeremiah 17:9 says,

> "The heart is deceitful above all things, and desperately wicked: who can know it?"

It is not unusual for thoughts such as 'My child could die,' 'My husband could marry another woman,' 'I could fail my exams,' 'Thieves could break into our house,' and 'I could lose my job' to pass through our minds. These things have not yet happened; nevertheless they get us worried. Dwelling on these thoughts affect our response to situations and we must decide to stop the flow of these evil thoughts. Don Herold said, "If I had my life to live over, I would perhaps have more actual troubles but I'd

Our actions are expressions of our thoughts. have fewer imaginary ones." You cannot think fear and act bold. They are two opposites. Our actions are expressions of our thoughts. When we think good thoughts we will act restful. Conversely, when our thoughts are bad, we will act worried.

Philippians 4:8 says,

> "Finally brethren, whatsoever things are true, whatsoever things are honest, whatsoever things are just, whatsoever things are pure, whatsoever things are lovely, whatsoever things are of good report; if there be any virtue and if there be any praise, think on these things."

This verse is the criteria for experiencing the kind of peace described in **verse 4** which says,

> "And the peace of God which passeth all understanding, shall keep your hearts and minds through Christ Jesus."

Fight the inner conflict and let good thoughts win. Evil thoughts make us doubt God and kill our faith in Him. Someone once said, *'Feed your faith and your doubts will starve to death.'* Also, if you feed your doubts, your faith will die. **James 1:6** says, *"...For the one who wavers (hesitates, doubts) is like the billowing surge out at sea that is blown hither and thither and tossed by the wind."* A doubtful person is blown about by worries and imagined troubles.

There is a constant fight between good and evil thoughts that come to our minds. Evil thoughts, like birds, fly over our heads daily but we must never allow them to build nests on our heads. Daily defying unwholesome thoughts will slowly but effectively paralyze their potency in our lives. Soak your mind in the promises of the scriptures. I met an elderly woman and while we were talking about the worries of life she commented that all the things she worried about when she was young never took place. Will I ever get a sound education? Will I get married? Will I have children? Will I ever grow old? She said that she got all these things and even more. She later commented that she wished that she had never worried about them.

At times, indecision could cause inner conflicts. Should I or should I not? Should I take this job or should I look elsewhere for something better? Is this man good enough to be my husband or is he pretending? I refer to this state as periods of tension. The tension is often very high in us and we are usually troubled and worried due to fear of making the wrong choices. However, like I wrote before, worrying is not the solution. Facing the facts, praying through and taking a firm decision in spite of all odds would stop the worry and ease the burden of carrying the problems in our minds. Besides, if in doubt, cool it and trust God.

We could also get anxious when we experience conflict of values. This happens when you have opposing desires. Your quest to know more of God is conflicting with your desire to be rich by all means. As Christians, we are not permitted to get rich by all means but by God's means. And if one does not have the patience which is paramount to acquiring godly riches, worry sets in. You want to be humble, yet you are concerned about the way people treat you. This could generate a lot of worries within you. Inner conflict sets in when you pursue two divergent goals or missions. Success in any enterprise demands focus and stability. However, focus becomes lacking when life's pursuits fail to find a point of convergence; when two desires are at cross purposes; when set standards have to be compromised to achieve a sub-standard success. These would lead to dissatisfaction within and tension without.

WRONG COMPANIONS

> "Be not deceived: evil communications corrupt good manners" (1 Corinthians 15:33).

Do not fellowship with people who do not share your values. Many people would never have had certain anxieties if they have not come in contact with certain men and women. When you move with the wrong people; the chronic worriers, the negative thinkers, the covetous, the discontent, you are courting worry. Paul told the Corinthian church,

> "Be ye not unequally yoked together with unbelievers: for what fellowship hath righteousness with unrighteousness? And what communion hath light with darkness?" (2 Corinthians 6:14)

The Psalmist says in **Psalm 1:1**,

> "Blessed (Happy, fortunate, prosperous and enviable) is the man who walks and lives not in the counsel of the ungodly (following their advice, their plans and purposes), nor stands (submissive and inactive) in the path where sinners walk, nor sits down (to relax and rest) where the scornful (and the mockers) gather" (AMP).

The kind of friends we keep make or mar us; they determine our successes and failures in life. Good friends build, encourage and lovingly rebuke you when you are going wrong. The Psalmist emphasized how fortunate a man could be if he does not associate with the wrong fellows. He would be happy because he would be doing the right things.

> The kind of friends we keep make or mar us; they determine our successes and failures in life.

Blessed is the man who lives not in the counsel of the ungodly! When an ungodly person counsels and advises you, it leads to problems and anxiety. You must learn to walk with the right set of people: men who are versed in the ways of the Lord; companions who can give you good advice based on the Word of God. Show me your friends and I will tell you who you are. Your friends could be great determinants in the course that your life takes. If you have friends who worry about everything, they will influence you into worrying too. But if your friends are positive, confess good things and see the good side of everything, they will lift up your spirit.

A pessimist, passing through a garden blooming with roses blamed God for putting thorns in the midst of roses while an optimist going through the same garden thanked God for putting roses in the midst of thorns. The world is what you say it is. Move with the right people and you will live right. Dinah, the daughter of Jacob was a lady who had the wrong companions and caused a lot of trouble by her actions. **Genesis 34:1** reads,

> **"And Dinah the daughter of Leah, which she bare unto Jacob went out to see the daughters of the land."**

Her friendship with the Canaanite daughters eventually led to her rape and created problems for Jacob and his household. Moving with the wrong people not only creates worries for you; it also puts those around you in difficulty. "Do not be fooled. Bad companions ruin good character" **(GNB).**

VICTIMS OF CIRCUMSTANCES

The events of September 11, 2001, brought worry in a new dimension to the nations of the world. The day dawned like any other in United States of America. Men and women rose up early to go about their daily businesses. When the workers in the twin towers of the World Trade Centre in New York City got to work that morning, many of them never knew that it was their last working day on earth. That day, nineteen terrorists, working in teams of four or five, hijacked four commercial jetliners and turned them toward targets chosen for destruction. Two of the planes, loaded with fuel and passengers, were flown at full speed into the twin towers. The buildings burst into flame and then collapsed, killing thousands. A third terrorist crew smashed their plane into the Pentagon, headquarters of the U.S. military in Arlington, Virginia.

The hijackers of the fourth airliner apparently intended to hit another target in the Washington, D.C., but passengers on the plane realized what was happening and fought back. This airplane crashed in a field in rural Pennsylvania. That day about three thousand people died and the world was shaken. Within the twinkle of an eye, worry, the public number one enemy reared up its head. People who had relations working in those towers were worried about their safety. Frantic phone calls were made. Nations got afraid and people walked in fear. The dread of another attack hung in the air. And many nations were left with the question: who will be next?

In December 2004, the worst tsunami disaster in history occurred, when an undersea earthquake, centered in the Indian Ocean generated an ocean wave that struck the coasts of 14 countries from Southeast Asia to northeastern Africa. The International Committee of the Red Cross reported that as a result of the tsunami over 250,000 people were left dead; with nearly two-thirds of the deaths occurring in Indonesia. High death tolls were also reported in India, Sri Lanka, and Thailand.

In 1995, the Los Angeles Times reported, "The western port city of Kobe remained virtually paralyzed today in the wake of the 7.2-magnitude earthquake that killed more than 2,000 people and sent as many as 120,000 persons seeking refuge. It laid waste to assurances that modern construction technology protects city dwellers in Japan from major seismic damage. In what ...was called Japan's most devastating tremor since the Great Tokyo Earthquake of 1923, police put the death toll at 2,014, with 1,058 missing and 11,977 injured. Most of the dead perished in their homes as the quake struck shortly before dawn Tuesday." This was superseded by the Haiti earthquake of 2010 which had left over three hundred thousand dead, many injured and maimed, and several hundreds of thousands homeless.

Certain things happen in our daily lives, which are beyond our control. These conditions could be spontaneous or gradual; nevertheless they create a form of tension for the individual or community affected. You may have your life well planned out; and then suddenly, something unusual occurs to disrupt your plans. A loved one dies, your benefactor loses his job. These kinds of events happen without notice and when they occur they induce anxiety, perplexities and despondency. Jesus predicted these times; He said,

> "For nation shall rise against nation, and kingdom against kingdom: and there shall be earthquakes in divers places, and there shall be

famines and troubles: these are the beginnings of sorrows" (Mark 13:8).

However, through all these, He told us,

"These things I have spoken unto you, that in me ye might have peace. In the world ye shall have tribulation: but be of good cheer; I have overcome the world" (John 16:33).

CONSEQUENCES OF OUR ACTION

Past actions could sometimes create worries for us. Many of us have done things without bearing the consequences of our actions in mind. **Galatians 6:7** says, *"Do not be deceived, God is not mocked; for whatever a man sows, that he will also reap."* Smokers could grow up to develop respiratory diseases like lung cancer or chronic obstructive pulmonary disease. This could cause a lot of discomfort, pain and worries.

Some parents in the bid to have a fulfilling career have sacrificed parental consciousness and responsibility. As a result of their negligence their children end up becoming drug addicts', gangsters, prostitutes, pregnant teenagers, committing abortion and developing complications; thus giving such parents lots of worries and heartaches.

Most of man's worry today result from his past deeds. G. W. Lyon says, 'Worry is the interest paid by those who borrow trouble.'

However, you cannot do anything about your past. The Lord says, *"For I will forgive their iniquity, and I will remember their sin no more"* **(Jeremiah 31:34).** Get over your past; resolve to start afresh and make a new focus for the future.

CONTACT WITH THE POWERS OF DARKNESS

Worry could result when one comes in contact with the powers of darkness. How do you come in contact with these powers? When you consult a clairvoyant, a sorcerer, or a prophet who claims he can turn your situation around. You are no longer interested in waiting for God's time; instead you create your own timeline. This is where problems start. The devil takes over and begins to control your life.

Proverbs 10:22 says,

> "The blessing of the LORD makes one rich, and He adds no sorrow with it" (NKJV).

However, when we court the devil, he gives us a lot of problems. Behind the devils glittering pleasures, is a hook. If you swallow his judicious offerings, you will be linked to the pains that accompany them. Signing a contract with the powers of darkness is equivalent to taking on a lifetime of perpetual anxiety.

When God's time becomes too slow for a man, he creates one which is so fast that it snuffs life out of him before he has barely lived it. God gives blessings without adding sorrows and troubles. His mill may grind slowly but it grinds surely. And His delays are never denials. He is the one who puts one in a position and gives peace, which transcends human understanding. When we go out of the shadow of His wings, we encounter the powers of darkness and these give us problems to worry about.

CHAPTER FOUR

CONSEQUENCES OF WORRY

> Worry distorts our thinking, disturbs our work, disquiets our soul, disturbs our body, and disfigures our face. It destroys our friends, demoralizes our life, defeats our faith and debilitates our energy.
>
> **William Arthur Ward**

Perhaps, you are still wondering, "Is it really possible to overcome worry?" I believe you will decide to take action if you know what worry does to your physical, mental and spiritual faculties and your life as a whole.

Someone once said, "Worry wastes today's time to

clutter up tomorrows opportunities with yesterday's trouble." Worry brings a lot of pain, both to the mind and the body; it is a disease that ravages both the rich and the poor, without discriminating between the literate and the illiterate. The consequences of worry are numerous. I hope that by the time you are through with this chapter you would be ready to drop your worries and start living.

Worry Initiates Misery

I once heard the story of a man who worried about everything. He worried because he was losing his hair, because he was too thin; because he might not marry the girl he loved; because he would never be rich enough to cater for his family; because he might never be a good father; because he was having stomach ulcer, because he felt he was not living fine. He worried about anything his mind could dwell upon and he became very miserable; so miserable that he could no longer go to work, talk to people or control his life. Every day to him was agony.

One day he decided to travel out of town to another city in search of happiness. As he boarded the train, his father gave him a letter with the instruction "Not to be opened until you get to your destination." On getting to the city, he opened the letter and it read, "Son, by the time you read this letter you would be several miles from home but you would not be feeling any different because the problem is not where you live but 'you.' It is not the circumstances but how you think about and react to them. As a man thinks in his heart, so he is."

> The problem is not where you live but 'you.'

That letter opened his eyes to how foolish he had been. He discovered that he did not have to change anything in the world to be happy; what needed changing was his mindset. He decided to stop worrying and went back home. Overnight his life changed. He later married the girl he wanted to marry and did very well in life. To overcome worry, what needs changing is our mindset.

Worry is belief in the negative, anticipation of tragedy and a sure recipe for failure. Worry and happiness are mutually exclusive. No one sows worry and reaps happiness. You either worry and are agitated or don't and be happy. Real joy does not come from external circumstances but from within; it is how you have trained your mind to respond to situations that determines how joyful you will be. It solely depends on your mental

> Real joy does not come from external circumstances but from within.

attitude. John Milton was an English poet and author, who was best known for his epic poem *Paradise Lost*. Although blind he did great things in his lifetime. In reflection he said, "The mind is its own place, and in itself can make a heaven of hell, and a hell of heaven." No matter what you have or who you are, you can never really experience peace until you have stopped worrying. Happiness or a worry-free life does not depend on the things you have acquired but on the internal milieu you have developed. **Proverbs 17:22** says,

> **"A happy heart is good medicine and a cheerful mind works healing but a broken spirit dries up the bones."**

A Jewish proverb says, "If you are bitter at heart, sugar in the mouth will not help you." In the same way, riches and degrees will not do anything to alleviate your misery if you are worried. Napoleon with all his power, riches and glory said, "I have never known six happy days in my life." And Eric Clapton said, "I can have all the money and cars in the world and be unhappy. Once you find out that money and fame and success doesn't do it, where do you go then? That's a big dilemma. I had all those things; a beautiful wife, cars, a home, money, friends. All the things that you think a man could need and it didn't stop me from drinking. I was depressed. I was suicidal." That is the effect of worry in the life of a man.

Worry ages us and makes us sour; it destroys our complexion, ruins our looks and forms wrinkles on our faces, it makes us look older than we actually are. Andrew Solomon, in his *Anatomy of Melancholy* wrote, "When you are depressed, the past and the future are absorbed entirely by the present as in the world of a three year old. You can neither remember feeling better or imagine that you will feel better... Depression means that you have no point of view." Worry fills your life with gloom.

Worry causes Mental Stress and Predisposes to all kinds of Diseases

An agitated and distraught mind depreciates the body. Worry generates tension and pressure within our body, puts stress on the brain and results into many mental illnesses. Mental institutions are getting filled up across the world and the reason has been attributed to worry. Statistics have shown that suicide rates are on the increase every year. People are no more weathering the storms of life; they are simply giving up!

Doctors have commented that seventy percent of complaints patients present with is insomnia. 'Doctor, I experience sleepless nights. I have an ulcer.' The underlying factor is worry. Many people today are sick in the body because their mind is sick. Plato, the ancient philosopher commented, "The greatest mistake physicians make is that they attempt to cure the body without attempting to cure the mind; yet the mind and body are one and should not be treated separately." Worry can drive a man crazy. It is a strain on our mental faculties. Dale Carnegie, in his book, *How to Stop Worrying and Start Living* said, "Worry is like the constant drip, drip, drip of water and the constant drip, drip, drip of worry often drives men to insanity and suicide."

It is a known fact that many mentally disturbed patients have been victims of worry, anxiety and fear. In *Worry- and How not to*, C. S. Clarke, wrote, "Worry as a stressor is a direct source of headaches, insomnia, ulcers and other gastric distress, paranoia, generalized anxiety disorders, depression and phobias. Most stress experts believe that it is an indirect source of disorders involving the immune system, such as cancer. We can literally worry ourselves to death. For example, when worry leads to depression and the depression becomes deep and unrelieved, our immune systems break down to the point where even a cold virus could become a killer."

Worry burdens us with impending but often unreal troubles. When the mind takes on too much pressure, the build-up affects the mind. Many have allowed both seen and unseen dilemmas weigh them down and affect them. Do you still want to maintain full control over your mental faculties? Then, quit worrying. Dr Alexis Carroll, said, "Those who keep the peace of their inner selves in the midst of the tumult of the modern city are immune from nervous diseases."

Most diseases are engendered by worry. Doctors talk about psychosomatic diseases. These are diseases which cannot be explained just by their physical manifestations but which have a psychological basics or a state of the mind, which contributes to it. This kind of disease plagues worriers. In his book, *Nervous Stomach*

> Ulcers frequently flare up or subside according to the hills and valleys of emotional stress.

Troubles, Dr. Joseph F. Montague, wrote, "You do not get ulcers from what you eat, you get ulcers from what is eating you." And Dr. W. C. Alvarez of Mayo Clinic said, "Ulcers frequently flare up or subside according to the hills and valleys of emotional stress." Worry creates tensions and predisposes us to high blood pressure or worsens an existing hypertension.

During the 2nd World War, many were shocked to hear that about three hundred and fifty thousand Americans had been killed in battle. But at exactly the same period, over one million people died of heart disease at home in USA and nobody noticed or raised any alarm. Worry and intense stress has been linked to heart diseases. A certain man, writing about worry and what it does, wrote, "Stress and worry break us down; they are the unseen sources of our headaches, backaches, heartaches, and bellyaches. They produce everything from obesity to obscenity, from constipation to diarrhoea, from impatience to impotence, they give us knotted stomach, sleepless nights, high blood pressure, low morale, they make our temper short and our days of bearing those tempers long, they cause indigestion, irritation, chest pain and muscles strain." Dr. Edward Podolsky, a reputable medical doctor in his book *'Stop Worrying and Get Well'* commented: "Worry causes heart trouble, high blood pressure, some forms of asthma, rheumatism, ulcers, cold, thyroid malfunction, arthritis, migraine headaches, blindness and a host of stomach disorders in addition to ulcers."

As a medical doctor, I know that many people become victims of ill health as a result of worry and unnecessary anxiety. To have a healthy body, you must have a healthy mind. A happy frame of mind goes a long way to give strength to the body. We once had a patient suffering from cancer. He was so worried that his condition deteriorated daily. One day, during the ward round, we encouraged him to cease from his worries and trust God. The man decided to abstain from worry and to his amazement, his health improved. He opted for a life of peace afterwards and his health remarkably improved. John Calvin, a man who was fond of always having anxiety before he changed, said, "Those who are prone to anxiety wear themselves out and become their own executioner." and Dr Alexis Carroll, a Nobel Prize winner in medicine says, "Businessmen who do not know how to fight worry, die young."

Are you suffering from certain diseases because you have overburdened your mind with worries? It is high time you got well; it is time you dropped your worries and opt for a life of peaceful communion with God. Anxiety cannot change your situation, it only worsens it.

Worry Amplifies the Problems

Worry magnifies the situation while it minimizes our strength. It exaggerates a minute problem and makes it more than it actually is. I know of a person who takes every examination with extreme anxiety. He would read and read and over read because he did not want to fail. He would not rest. Most times, when his colleagues go out to relax, he would continue reading. Eventually, he developed severe abdominal pain prior to a major examination. He was urged to focus on his health but he would not listen. Soon his condition deteriorated and he had to go for surgery. He became extremely worried because he knew the surgery would not allow him to prepare well for the examination. Rather than concentrate on his health, he kept on reading on the sick bed. In the end, I heard that this young man developed complications that later resulted in his death.

Worry makes a mountain out of our problems and makes us expend our energy in an unwise way. It turns life's challenges to roadblocks and blinds us to possibilities in our difficulties. Obstacles are stepping-stones to greater opportunities. But when we entertain worry, we cloud today's prospects with tomorrow problems. Worry puts fear into us, hampers our abilities to fight back and gets us muddled up in the problems we fear. You can either decide to worry or settle down to think about your next line of action. The situation might not be as bad as worry makes it; you need to harness all your strength to meet whatever is coming your way.

Worry does not fix anything; it only adds an extra weight to any problem. It clouds the mind, wrecks your emotions and kills the spirit. How does a perplexed, tensed, and agitated person accomplish anything worthwhile? Corrie Ten Boom, a Dutch Christian Holocaust survivor who

> Worry does not fix anything; it only adds an extra weight to any problem.

helped many Jews escape during the World War II wrote, "Worry does not empty tomorrow of its trouble; it empties today of its strength." You can overcome any problem if you can stop worrying. God has given every man an inherent capacity to win over any situation and when we magnify the situations at the expense of the resources available to us, we fail. "Worry," says a Swedish proverb, "often gives a small thing a big shadow."

Worry victimizes us

One of the ways by which the powers of darkness work is to manipulate your worries in order to victimize you. When a sorcerer notices your anxiety, he finds a prophecy to suit it. Get worried about your child, and you will receive a prophecy that the child will die unless you do something. Get anxious about your examinations and you will receive a prophecy that you will fail. If you worry about your car, the prophecy could be an impending accident. Worry becomes a potential loophole through which clairvoyants manipulate us and destroy our convictions.

CONSEQUENCES OF WORRY

Worry makes you susceptible to the wiles of evil men. Several people had become victim of fraudsters. Sometimes ago, I was about travelling out of the country, when an old acquaintance invited me to his house. When I got there, he tried cajoling me into some shady investments. After talking for a while, I got an inkling of what he was trying to say, got very annoyed and threatened to arrest him. When I got to that house the next day, he had disappeared. If I had been so worried about being rich, he would have duped me. Worry enables deceitful men to capitalize on your presumed troubles and bring you to despair.

Worry Drains our Energy

Worry dissipates our energy into non-essentials; things that don't really matter. Many of us waste our strength on trivialities. Jesus told Martha in **Luke 10:41-42,**

> "Martha, Martha, you are anxious and troubled about many things. There is need of only one but a few things. Mary has chosen the good portion (that which is to her advantage) which shall not be taken away from her."

Martha was so worried about Jesus' upkeep that she

missed out on the essence of his presence. But Mary chose the best; she did not spend her energy on things that will not last. She chose the valuable option of learning at Jesus' feet. She chose to expend her energy with wisdom; she chose peace of mind.

Friend, what have you chosen? Is it to worry over matters, which are unimportant? Is it to expend your energy on trifles? *Worry is like a rocking chair. It gives you something to do but does not get you anywhere.*

Worry Mars our Faith

Worry is one of the greatest expressions of doubt; it is faith in the negative. A song writer wrote 'Why worry when you can pray' and I changed it to, 'Why worry when you have faith.' Rather than concentrate on the promises of God, many concentrate on the problems at hand; rather than trusting God, they are busy analyzing the trials they are going through. Most times, we exercise worry, when we expect something from God and those things do not come quickly. However, we need to know that God's time is always on time. He could be a slow strategist but he acts speedily. His time is the best for us. A. J. Gordon, American Baptist Preacher and theologian said, "The promises of God are certain but they do not all mature in days." It could take years but surely they will come.

In worry, we question God's integrity and dispute His ability to actualize His words. Indirectly, we are saying we believe neither His word nor his promises. **1 John 5:10** says,

> "**He who believes in the Son of God has the witness in himself; he who does not believe God has made Him a liar, because he has not believed the testimony that God has given of His Son.**"

To which Paul replied in **Romans 3:4**,

> "**God forbid: yea, let God be true, but every man a liar...**"

As previously remarked, "Worry is putting question marks where God has put periods" (John R. Rice). The Dake's Annotated Reference Bible commentator wrote, "Worrying is foolish, for whatever is going to happen cannot be stopped by worry and if it does not happen there is really nothing to worry about. Should adversities actually come one may still be victorious by trusting in God."

In *Transformed by Thorns*, Dr. E. Stanley Jones commented, "I am inwardly fashioned for faith, not for fear. Fear is not my native land; faith is. I am so made that worry and anxiety are sand in the machinery of life; faith is the oil. I live better by faith and confidence than by fear, doubt and anxiety. In anxiety and worry, my being is gasping for breath--these are not my native air. But in faith and confidence, I breathe freely--these are my native air. A John Hopkins University doctor says, "We do not know why it is that worriers die sooner than the non- worriers, but that is a fact. But I, who am simple of mind, think I know; we are inwardly constructed in nerve and tissue, brain cell and soul, for faith and not for fear. God made us that way. To live by worry is to live against reality."

Worry Questions the Efficacy of God's Word

Hebrew 11:1 says,

> 'Now faith is the assurance (the confirmation, the title deed) of the things we hope for, being the proof of things we do not see and the conviction of their reality (faith perceiving as real fact what is not revealed to the senses)' (AMP).

I like the latter end of that verse which says, "...faith is perceiving as real fact what is not revealed to the senses." Faith does not look at the facts on ground; these are the things our senses can understand. Faith is beyond our human senses, it simply believes God. An unknown writer noted, "The beginning of anxiety is the end of faith, and the beginning of true faith is the end of anxiety."

The story was told of George Muller Massena, one of Napoleon's generals, who suddenly appeared with 18,000 soldiers before an Austrian town which had no means of defending itself. The town council met, certain that capitulation was the only answer. The old dean of the church reminded the council that it was Easter, and begged them to hold services as usual and to leave the trouble in God's hands. They followed his advice. The dean went to the church and rang the bells to announce the service. The French soldiers heard the church bells ring and concluded that the Austrian army had come to rescue the town. They broke camp, and before the bells had ceased ringing, vanished.

Do you still pray to God about your problems? Do you still believe He is the God of all possibilities? If you really desire to grow in the knowledge of God, you have to cease from worry. Norman Vincent Peale, the great Christian teacher and author who wrote *The Normal Christian Living* says, *"Worry is a destructive process of occupying the mind with thoughts contrary to God's love and care."* Drop your worry and grab your faith.

Worry Initiates Marital Disharmony

Worry is the major cause of separation, rancour, cacophonous homes, miserable wives, depressed husbands and dispirited children. Many parents are anxious rather than being thankful. They worry about petty issues rather than being purposeful and they have mutual expectation instead of mutual acceptance. Worry prevents mutual understanding and causes irreparable damage to homes. Due to different backgrounds and ways of upbringing, several spouses disagree on several issues and this result in unnecessary worry. A worried man is tense and resentful. This rubs on the wife who takes it out on the children. Worry stunts the growth of love in the home. It turns the home to battle grounds where word missiles are thrown, and the victims of this unjust war are the children. They are deprived of peace, love, and strength necessary to face life challenges.

Richard T. Colgan in his article *Stuttering- Signal to Emotional Stress* wrote the moving story of a young girl called Janet: 'Janet was five years old when her parents, concerned over her inability to pronounce certain words and syllables, took her to the family physician. He told them not to worry; she would outgrow it. However, a year later, when Janet experienced respiratory difficulties complicated by violent and sudden contractions of the throat and face muscles, her parents sought out another doctor. He prescribed garlic, onions and strong food to strengthen her speech followed by a series of periodic visitations designed to assist her

> Worry stunts the growth of love in the home.

'increase her will power in order to make her master herself.' Today Janet is a chronic stutterer, bewildered by her problem and totally frightened of mixing in society, even with small neighbourly groups. The conflict in her home has generated an ailment she finds hard to overcome. Had her parents known, or had the medical advice sought out to investigate the emotional stresses and tension within the family environment, perhaps she would have overcome the problem and become a more secure, self-confident and friendly person."

Janet's problem is not unique. Many children are bearing the brunt of unstable homes and unfriendly family environment. Several cases of autism, stuttering, drug abuse, teenage pregnancies, alcoholism, prostitution, gangsterism and suicide among teenagers result from worry-ridden homes. The children, in looking for ways to drown their pain and anxieties, take to vices. Worriers are like carriers of infectious disease. They infect others and spread the scourge. Just as diseases weaken the body, so also worry breaks the home until it results in separation.

Worry Makes us Miss out on God

Are you worrying as a Christian? Then, you are missing

some very important things. Worry is a form of atheism. It enthrones itself in the place of God. An atheist is not only a person who says there is no God; he also behaves as if God does not care. In worrying, you miss out on God's power. When you stop worrying, you testify to the existence of a supreme God who has all power in His hands and has the control over all that happens in your life. And once you acknowledge this fact, he steps into the situation and stills the storm.

> Worry makes you anticipate troubles, which seldom come to those who trust God.

Worry makes you anticipate troubles, which seldom come to those who trust God. God has seen the end from the beginning. He knows the destination and is prepared to take you there. **Romans 8:28** says, *"And we know that all things work together for good to them that love God, to them who are called according to his purpose."* All things! That is your past, present, pains and pitfalls are working together for a wonderful future. Christ in you is the hope of glory! Worry makes us to miss out on the glory and goodness of God. He has given us a command, a rule which is binding: do not worry! But when you worry, you lose all the benefits that accompany obedience. It is a sin! One cannot be in sin and expect the blessings of God to abound. You have to choose between worrying and trusting. The story was told of the response of Martin Luther's wife to him on one of his worrying days. She dressed in black all day. Martin asked her, "Why are you putting on dark clothes?" She replied, "Since you are worrying, then God must be dead!"

The Bible constantly reminds us of God's ability to see us through life's problems. He is the all seeing and never-failing God. He loves us and cares for us. However, for us to fully enjoy His provisions we have to live in obedience. In Isaiah 1:19, He said, 'If ye be willing and obedient, ye shall eat the good of the land'. Are you ready to obey the Word and gain the riches that come from God? Do you want to eat the good of the land? Are you aware that there are some problems, which are beyond your human power to solve? Epicteus, a Greek philosopher had this to say: "There is only one way to happiness and that is to cease worrying about things beyond the power of our will." Don't be anxious about your future. God is already there.

THE PROFESSIONAL WORRIER

"I have a mountain of credit card debt," one man told another,

'I have lost my job, my car is being repossessed and our house is in foreclosure, but I'm not worried about it'

"Not worried about it!" exclaimed his friend.

"No, I've hired a professional worrier. He does all my worrying for me, and that way I don't have to think about it."

"That's fantastic. How much does your professional worrier charge for his services?"

"Fifty thousand dollars a year."

"Where are you going to get that kind of money?' asked his astonished friend.

"I don't know," came the reply, "That's his worry."

In a sense the Lord's servants do have a professional worrier to do all their worrying for them. As **1 Peter 5:7** says, *"You can throw the whole weight of your anxieties upon Him, for you are His personal concern."* (Phillips)

(Culled from Nelson's complete book of stories, illustrations and quotes)

CHAPTER FIVE

HOW TO HANDLE WORRY

> Said the robin to the sparrow,
> I should really like to know,
> Why these anxious human beings,
> Rush about and worry so.
> Said the sparrow to the robin,
> I think that it must be,
> They have no heavenly father,
> Such as cares for you and me.
> **Anonymous**

Are we aware of the presence of a heavenly father who cares for us? If so, do we acknowledge his ability to take our worries upon him? If God could provide for little creatures, how much more we, who are created in His own image? Jesus says,

"Look at the birds, free and unfettered, not tied down to a job description, careless in the care of God. And you count far more to him than birds" (Matthew 6:26).

Until we begin to make efforts to stop worry and anxiety in our lives, we have not started living. Worry like every other habit can be conquered; we can live in peace within ourselves. In this chapter, we shall be looking at some principles, which will enable us to handle efficiently and possibly erase every form of anxiety from our lives. These principles, if put into action, will enhance our relationship with God and will open our eyes to see that today's worries are like puddles, which by tomorrow will have dried up.

ANALYZE WHY YOU WERE WORRIED

"Confusion is the chief cause of worry," says the late Herbert E. Hawkes who was Dean of Columbia College, Columbia University for twenty-two years. When a man gets confused, he complicates the issue. It is only in analyzing the facts that you can get to the root of the problem. Get the facts, face them and examine them. With

> Confusion is the chief cause of worry

examination and analysis comes the light of knowledge; with it comes the understanding of what caused your worry and the wisdom to deal with the situation. Many people blame their worries on someone else. 'My boss got me into all these problems. If he had not sacked me, I would not be worrying about finances.' Have you asked yourself the reasons why you were sacked? Do you think your attitude to your work could have contributed to your boss' action? Would that attitude, if not changed, affect your future job opportunities? What can you do to enhance your skills?

Someone once said, "The secret of happiness is to learn to accept the impossible, to do without the indispensable and to bear the intolerable." In every one of us is an inherent power to deal with our own situations. Analyze why you are in that situation. While trying to collect facts, try to keep your emotions in check. If possible put them in writing. Write a list of your worries, ask questions on it, and do a detailed examination of the list. Writing it down relieves your heart of the burden and enables you to face it. An elderly woman, reminiscing on how she handled her worries, said that when she was younger she was always worried. One day, she decided to analyze her worries and she wrote the list of all the things worrying her, locked it in a wardrobe and forgot about it. In short, she locked away her problems. Thirty years later, she was clearing out junk when she discovered that list under a pile of old books. She found that everything that she worried about in that list never came to pass. To worry is unnecessary.

A problem fully examined is a problem almost solved. When we analyze a problem, we soon realize there is not much to worry about in it. Unless you get the facts, you cannot attempt finding the solution. Take time to put it down, put it under close scrutiny and you will either discard it or decide on it.

ACT ON WHAT YOU CAN

With analysis comes decision. This decision is implemented in action. There are certain situations, which you can act upon. Putting yourself into action automatically puts your mind off your worry. If you are worried about owning a car or a house, make a plan of action. Set a plan, a programme or a time schedule on what you have to do about your problems. Then, act on them. Don't just fold your hands. When you set things in motion, worry takes the way out. Pythagoras, the great mathematician said, "Concern should drive us into action and not into a depression. No man is free who cannot control himself." Do you want to be free? Get something doing.

> Concern should drive us into action and not into a depression.

When you get busy, you stop worrying. Someone gave an antidote for worry. He said, "Doing beats stewing. When you are tempted to fret and worry, divert your energy. Don't sit around with the curtains drawn wringing your hands. Throw open the window, find something that needs to be done and get busy." Get involved in something that will keep your mind and body occupied. During the height of World War II, someone asked Winston Churchill if he worried about his tremendous responsibilities and he said, "I am too busy. I have no time for worry." A busy person has got no time to worry. Inaction is a fresh garden in which worry grows.

Analysis without action is useless. It is like going about in circles; you still come back to where you started from. "To look is one thing. To see what you look at is another. To understand what you see is a third. To learn from what you understand is still something else. But to act on what you learn is all that really matters" (Bits and Pieces). **James 1:22** says,

> **"But be ye doers of the word, and not hearers only, deceiving your own selves." (KJV)**

Act on what you have concluded upon and do not look back. Damn the consequences and act, by the time you start doubting your actions, fear will come upon you and you will become jittery. Stop looking over your shoulder. Williams James, the American psychologist said, "When once a decision is reached and execution is the order of the day, dismiss absolutely all responsibility and care about the outcome." Action puts you on the move. It pushes you forward. Even if you are on the right track you will get run over if you just sit there. You have to keep going. Aldous Huxley said, "The great end of life is not knowledge but action." Do something about your anxieties. Do not just sit there, pacing up and down. Unless you carry out your action, all your fact-finding, questioning and analysis will be a waste of time and energy. Do not hesitate, just go ahead and do it. Leonardo da Vinci said, "Iron rusts from disuse, water loses its purity from stagnation and in cold weather become frozen; so inaction saps the vigour of the mind."

'Keep busy' is one of the best prescriptions for worried minds. Why? You cannot effectively think of more than one particular thing at a time. So if you get absorbed in something that will require both your mental and physical abilities, you would not worry. In indolence there is perpetual despondency. Stop being idle, it increases your worry rate. Take a book and read. Get yourself involved in research work. Find a way of reaching out to others. Help people who are less privileged. Rather than grumbling about your condition, think of a way of improving the lives of others. Someone said, "Master the art of altruism and become genuinely interested in people around you. Your genuine interest in other people will assassinate the master of worry."

> In indolence there is perpetual despondency. Stop being idle, it increases your worry rate.

When you swing into action, you lose the habit of worry. This form of treatment is called 'occupational therapy.' James L. Mursell, a professor of education in Columbia said, "Worry is most apt to ride you ragged, not when you are in action, but when the day's work is done. Your imagination can run riot then and bring up all sorts of ridiculous possibilities and magnify each little blunder. At such a time your mind is like a motor operating without its load. It races and threatens to burn out its bearings or even to tear itself to bits. The remedy for worry is to get completely occupied doing something constructive." Lay your hands on something; put your mind in it and before you know, worry would have been completely removed.

ACCEPT WHAT YOU CANNOT CHANGE

Now, there are some things that we cannot change no matter how hard we try. Worrying over them is absolutely irrational. You have to accept them and move on with your life. A loved one had died; you cannot bring him back. No matter how unfortunate you feel about your race, you cannot change it. Your parents will still be your parents. If you have a physical disability, you have to live with it. These are few among all the innumerable things you cannot change. You have to develop the courage to accept these things.

We would meet some unavoidable situations as we go through life. Though we start out life with high optimisms and lofty ideas, yet fate has a way of dealing with us in ways we least expect. When this occurs, we have to learn to adapt. As one goes through various challenges and gains from experience, one discovers that things may neither turn out as well as one anticipated nor as badly as one feared. We can accept the inevitable and develop fortitude against it or we can destroy our lives with worry and bitterness. William James, a great philosopher said, "Be willing to have it so. Acceptance of what has happened is the first step to overcoming the consequences of any misfortune." Was it an accident that got you maimed? You can still make something out of your life, if only you would stop being bitter and face your misfortune bravely. I like a popular prayer written by Dr. Reinhold Neibuhr several years ago. It says:

God grant me the serenity
To accept the things I cannot change,
The courage to change the things I can;
And the wisdom to know the difference.

There are certain situations, which cannot be changed.

At such times, God usually gives us an inner strength to adapt to it. Joseph would not have liked being sold into slavery. But he had no choice. He could not have liked being sent to prison for an offence he did not commit. He also had no choice in that matter. But out of that situation he received an inner strength from God, which sustained him throughout his stay there and took him out of the prison to the King's Palace. In fact, certain things happen so that God can lift us up. But we need wisdom to see that we have to adapt to these things and make the most of what we have. Things always turn out best for those who make the best out of the way things turn out! It is just a little that God needs to make us great. I usually say that *"Out of the broken pieces of the past, God can make an edifice of hope."*

> Things always turn out best for those who make the best out of the way things turn out!

Joseph adapted himself to prison life so well that he became the head of the prisoners. He made maximum use of his ability by using his gift of interpretation of dreams and this made him the Prime Minister in Egypt **(Genesis 37-41).** David adapted to the hatred he got from Saul, faced the challenges and out of that situation, God made him King of Judah and Israel **(1 Samuel 18:11- 2 Samuel 2:4).** Jesus adapted himself to God's will. He said, *"Father, if you are willing, take this cup from me; yet not my will but yours be done"* **(Luke 22:42 NIV).** He could have worried about the sufferings and resisted the Cross but he cooperated with the inevitable and went through the pains of Calvary. God lifted him up and now he is seated at the right hand of God.

It is not God's will that you should be sick. The bible says that He heals our infirmities. It is not God's will for you to be miserable but there are certain circumstances in your life to which God wants you to adapt and which by doing so, you receive the courage that allows you to win over that situation. You can even turn your situation to success. Beethoven composed better music than his contemporaries in spite of being deaf. The failures of Abraham Lincoln helped him to develop an undaunted determination and this carried him on till he became the President of America.

Are you maximizing your condition or are you worried about it? What cannot be changed has to be accepted.

We must learn to bear lightly what must be borne and remove all anxieties from our minds.

CHANGE YOUR ATTITUDE

Attitude is the way you see things, your response to an event, your behaviour towards it. It is your perception of a particular matter. Your attitude is the mirror through which you see situations and what you mirror in your mind is reflected in your life. It is your thought pattern. Not occasionally, you may hear somebody saying, 'This is the way I see it. This is how I feel about it.' Our attitudes about joy and misery have been well documented in history as potential weapons in the determination of our destiny.

In the Old Testament, King Solomon said,

> "For as he thinketh in his heart, so is he" (Proverbs 23:7).

William James, a renowned American Psychologist said, "The greatest discovery of my generation is that human beings can alter their lives by altering their attitudes." Regardless of your situation, you can change many things by changing your attitude towards them. Our mental attitude determines several things about our lives. If we think good thoughts we will live a good life. The same applies to bad and negative thoughts; that life would be filled with negativity. You are what you think you are. If sickly thoughts pervade your heart, you would probably become ill.

A great man, Viktor Frankl, suffered a lot during the Second World War in the hands of the Nazis. He went through agonies and torment at the concentration camp and many thought that after surviving the torture, he would become a defeated, marred and miserable person. But it was otherwise; he made a very important statement when he said, "Everything can be taken away from a man but one thing; the last of the human freedom, one's ability to choose one's attitude in any given set of circumstances." Viktor chose to be happy and to live a good life in spite of all he had gone through and like Jesus said of Mary, Viktor has chosen that good part, it shall not be taken away from him!

> You are what you think you are.

You can lose your money, clothes, properties and even parts of your body, however one thing remains with you:

your choice of reaction. Between action and reaction, there is a wide range of choice and you get what you choose. Your choice is very important! You could decide to shelve your worries and live a cheerful life. Look for the opportunities arising from your problems and maximize them. Abraham Lincoln, one of the greatest American Presidents who ever ruled said, "A man is about as happy as he makes up his mind to be." Nobody can make you sad except by your own permission.

Some people blame their misfortunes on others. 'I would have lived a fulfilled life if not for this malformed child.' Two people faced the same set of circumstances one emerged a victim while the other came out, a victor. Two prisoners looked out the prison door, one saw the sand on the ground, the other saw the stars in the sky. What made the difference? Their attitude. Clement Stone said, "There is little difference in people but that little difference makes a big difference. The little difference is attitude. The big difference is whether it is positive or negative." A person with a positive mental attitude looks at his predicament and gives thanks while another with a negative mental

> When you think right, things tend to work out right, for you.

attitude sees it and worries.

When you think right, things tend to work out right, for you. It has been said, "Nothing can stop the man with a right mental attitude from realizing his dreams. However, nothing on earth can help the man with a wrong mental attitude." A man with a wrong attitude has sentenced himself to destruction. Unless he changes, nothing can be done to save him. Get a businessman who feels he cannot succeed in business. Give him enough money to start something real big; he still would not succeed. Why? Success is far from his mind. Do you usually make the best use of the way things turn in your life? When you look at the ground what do you see? Is it ordinary sand of no value or stepping-stones to greatness?

Being worried about a situation is a wrong approach to its solution. Change your attitude towards the problem. I saw a write-up several years ago and I will like to share it with you. It said: "Age is more a matter of focus and physiology than chronology. Many people have lived many years but still have a skip in their walk and flexibility in their thought. A simple example of this is found on a rainy day. When "Old" people see a puddle, what do they do? They not only walk around it, they complain the whole time! On the other hand, children and those still young at heart might jump right in, laugh, splash around, and have a good time. Enjoy life's "Puddle." Live with a spring in your step, a smile on your face. Make cheerfulness, outrageousness and playfulness new priorities for your life. You're alive! You can feel good for no reason at all."

What caught my attention was the attitude of the old and the young. The "Old" saw the puddle as a misfortune while the young saw it as a means of adventure. It is quite disheartening to realize that many people today are living with the "Old" mentality. They are ruining the life that had barely begun by their attitude. Why don't you emulate the 'Young' in this article by laughing at the things causing you to worry? You will be surprised at how fast the tension will be reduced. In your mind you can become the healthiest, happiest person who has ever lived. It's just about changing your outlook concerning certain things.

Your mind can take you to the pinnacle of history and it can also make you a mediocre. One person listens to a sermon and exclaimed, 'Oh! What a wonderful sermon' and another listens to the same sermon and complained,

'What a wearying sermon.' One person listens to a piece of music and he gets excited, another listens to it and condemns it. The difference is their thought life. Our existence is what our thoughts make it. James Allen, a man who wrote the book 'As a man thinketh' that had sold millions wrote: "A man will find that as he alters his thoughts toward things and other people, things and other people will alter towards him." Life is like an echo, shout out and it will shout back at you. Think right and your life will be right. Think of evil things and your life will reflect evil.

> Life is like an echo, shout out and it will shout back at you. Think right and your life will be right.

Several methods have been described to ensure an attitudinal change but three basic principles will be discussed here.

Pause and praise: Count your blessings. There are so many things to be thankful for. Think of all the good things that have come your way. Be thankful for being alive. It has been said, "The secret of happiness is to count your blessings while others are adding up their troubles." Think and thank, it throttles worry. Have a thankful and positive mental disposition. Take a pause, look around you and take an inventory of the good things you see. Someone said, 'I had the blues because I had no shoes until upon the street I met a man who had no feet.' In counting your blessings, you do not only have to think of your possessions. Think of the free gifts of life. Have you thought of the free oxygen supply? The daily sunrise? The ever-present guard who stays awake while you sleep through the night? The gift of your sense? In fact, there are too many things to thank God for, if only you can think.

> Think and thank, it throttles worry.

Charles Spurgeon, one of the greatest eighteenth century preachers wrote of a man who broke his hip in an accident and got crippled. I believe this is one of several things that could dampen a young man's morale. Perhaps he had planned to be a pilot or a businessman. But fate had handed him crutches. Maybe his fiancee did not like the idea of a crippled husband. She might have left him in his troubles. A thousand and one things could have resulted in worry for him. But he had not seen the worst yet. The people of God decided to come around to pray for him and shortly after that another tragedy struck

- he fell and broke his hip again. Things had really reached the peak now. He would have thought of the long weeks he would be spending in the hospital waiting for the leg to get healed again, He could have been clenching his fist at God in anger and asking, 'God, why me.' But this young man never grew bitter. He and those with him kept on thanking God for his goodness and kindness. The result was that this time, the hip was set properly and he was able to walk without a limp again. The supposed tragedy was a blessing in disguise. Count your blessings.

Learn to think so that you can thank. If possible, put it down in writing. It gives you a better sense of appreciation. Are things going wrong? Praise God for those things that are still right. Are you going bankrupt? Thank God you are alive. When you dwell on the blessings, you would experience a change in attitude and thus eliminate worry.

Preach to yourself: Encourage yourself. Say good things to yourself. Remind yourself that life is a book that has not been concluded. You can still make it in the time left. Do not put a full stop when God has not. Do not conclude when God is yet to begin and do not end the book when He is just starting another chapter. Tell yourself you are good looking, though half of your face might have been scarred by fire. What matters is how you see yourself; what others say does not matter. Search for the good things in you and proclaim it. Are you discouraged? Encourage yourself.

Habakkuk was a prophet who recognized what it meant to preach to oneself and maximized it.

In **Habakkuk 3:17-18**, he said,

> "Although the fig tree shall not blossom, neither shall fruit be in the vines; the labour of the olive shall fail and the field shall yield no meat; the flock shall be cut off from the fold and there shall be no herd in the stalls. Yet I will rejoice in the Lord, I will rejoice in the God of my salvation."

This is like experiencing a six-fold failure. He could have chosen to worry himself to death over them. Yet he chose to rejoice. He preached to himself and he received strength. Verse 19 says, *"The Lord God is my strength and he will make me to walk upon mine high places..."* Preaching to oneself changes one's attitude to the problem and cuts worry short before it takes root.

Think of the promises not the problems: You can change your outlook by thinking about God's promises. Problems are challenges, which are not supposed to put us down but to make us strong enough to receive the promises of God. You don't have to dwell on the problems; dwell on the Word of God. His Word will be fulfilled in your life if you believe and receive it into your heart. When you are in Christ, His promises renew you.

"Therefore if any person is (in grafted) in Christ (the Messiah) he is a new creation" (2Corinthians 5:17 AMP).

Your mind becomes renewed and your perception changes. When you believe in God's promises, worry fades into the past. **2 Corinthians 1:20** says, *"For all the promises of God in him are yea and in him Amen, unto the glory of God by us."* The words of God are always truthful. He will fulfil them in our lives if we believe them. So we have to soak ourselves in these promises in order to overcome present overbearing circumstances.

You can change your situation by a change of attitude. The words of Lou Hotz readily come to mind: "Ability is what you are capable of doing. Motivation determines what you do. Attitude determines how well you do it." How well does your attitude permit you to overcome worry? When the condition seems impossible, that is when you need God.

CONTROL YOUR MOODS

In life, no matter how wonderful we are, our moods will set the tone for our lives. It will determine how high we can go or how far we will fall and that is why we must take steps to study our moods. Our moods are our feelings, our reaction to the events around us; they are not the events themselves. Whenever we are confronted with issues, the way we react to these events determine our moods; if we react in a negative manner to the things that happen to us, then we shall be pessimistic in our mind set. But if we have an optimistic mindset, regardless of what happens to us we will always reason from a positive outlook. The truth is that no matter how grievous events are, they are neutral. It is our reaction that give these events their significance. And our response to issues will determine whether we will be worried or not.

> No matter how grievous events are, they are neutral. It is our reaction that give these events their significance.

Apostle Paul was a man who developed a philosophy of life that he would not be moved, no matter the situation in which he found himself. **Philippians 4:11-13** says,

> "Actually, I don't have a sense of needing anything personally. I've learned by now to be quite content whatever my circumstances. I'm just as happy with little as with much, with much as with little. I've found the recipe for being happy whether full or hungry, hands full or hands empty. Whatever I have, wherever I am, I can make it through anything in the One who makes me who I am" (THE MSG).

I am certain that Paul knew that circumstances are very variable. That today he could be hungry and tomorrow he could be well fed. However, he decided that he would not allow his moods to be controlled by the circumstances around him. Perhaps Paul had seen how moods could destroy people's vision and mission. Some of us heard about one great Senator in America who was contesting for a public office. This man was highly rated by almost all the polls in America as the most likely candidate to win. However in one of his debates, he broke down in tears. The newspapers and television stations spread the news all over the nation and overnight the tables turned. People started asking: 'Can a senator, who cries under pressure be trusted to rule the country?' That was how the man lost his candidature and the election.

We saw the case of Moses; this was a man that God anointed and called to bring His people to the Promised Land. The Bible testified, *"Now the man Moses was very meek, above all the men which were upon the face of the earth"* **(Numbers 12:3)**. Moses was special to God; he spent 40 days and nights in His presence. When you talk about the laws of the world, most were derived from the canon laws that were brought forth by Moses. But when Moses saw the actions of the Israelites, he acted in anger and disobeyed God's instruction. **Numbers 20:11-12** records:

> "And Moses lifted up his hand, and with his rod he smote the rock twice: and the water came out abundantly, and the congregation drank, and their beasts also. And the LORD spake unto Moses and Aaron, Because ye believed me not, to sanctify me in the eyes of the children of Israel, therefore ye shall not bring this

congregation into the land which I have given them."

As a result, God told him he will not enter into the Promised Land. God did not even talk about the people of Israel; He did not talk about their stubbornness. However, the reaction of Moses robbed him of the glory of God. Can you see that how you control your moods can determine whether you will be exonerated or penalized?

We must never allow our actions to be governed by our moods. Whenever you are faced with circumstances in life, you enter into what I call an internal dialogue. The aftermath of that internal dialogue will produce your response to that situation. For instance, if somebody calls you a fool, that information is fed into your mind. You will then have an internal conversation with that word (Am I really a fool? What does this person mean? How should I react?) Your reaction to that man's statement will be dependent on what the internal dialogue arrives at.

> Choose your reaction rather than allow the events dictate your actions.

Out of that internal dialogue you can produce a blessing or a curse. Through your internal dialogue, you must learn to say no to certain worries, anxieties, depression and events that will destabilize you. Choose your reaction rather than allow the events dictate your actions.

Keep your mind on the mission: The Hebrew writer emphasized: *"Keep your eyes on Jesus, who both began and finished this race we're in. Study how he did it. Because he never lost sight of where he was headed--that exhilarating finish in and with God--he could put up with anything along the way: cross, shame, whatever. And now he's there, in the place of honor, right alongside God"* **(Hebrews 12:2 THE MSG).** When situations are not favourable and you are tempted to worry about it, keep your eyes on Jesus. When you are faced with conflicts within and troubles without, keep your eyes on Jesus. He said, "Study how he did it because he never lost sight of where he was headed." If Moses had not lost sight of where he was headed, he could have gotten to the Promised Land. Jesus never lost sight of the goal and He finished well. "When you find yourselves flagging in your faith, go over that story again, item by item, that long litany of hostility he plowed through. That will shoot adrenaline into your souls!" **(Hebrews 12:3 MSG)**

Jesus Christ looked at the finish line; He looked at the mission God had committed to Him and because of that He could put up with shame, curses, discomforts and whatsoever came His way. Rather than worry about the problems He had to face, He concentrated on the goal. Endure all it takes, go through the pains but never miss out on the mission. People who allow their moods to control them focus on the present conditions, exaggerate the problems, publicize the situation and lose out on the mission. Never settle in the present conditions; never let your worries distract you. If you will get your mood under control, you must keep your mind on the mission God has given you.

> Endure all it takes, go through the pains but never miss out on the mission.

Be bonded with Christ: How could Paul put up with every situation? Why was he not disturbed and worried about the chains that awaited him in ministry? Here lies the secret: *"I can do all things through Christ who strengthens me."* **(Philippians 4:13)** He was ready for anything, equal to any task through Him who infused him with inner strength. Can I endure this uncaring attitude from my loved ones? Yes you can because you have been empowered by Christ who infuses strength in you. Can I take this maltreatment from my boss? Yes, I can because Christ infuses strength in me. **Ephesians 6:10** says, *"In conclusion, be strong in the Lord, be empowered through your union with him, draw your strength from him, (that strength which His boundless might provides)"* **(AMP).**

Because you are bonded to Christ and in union with Him, you can put up with anything; you can face any situation. Your relationship with your spouse or with your boss is a temporary relationship, but your relationship with Christ is boundless; you can rise above anything through your union with Him. Someone asked, "How can I survive if this plan fails?" God always has a Plan B. He is building our lives after a particular pattern. As your plans face insurmountable conditions, God is rolling out another plan. As children of God, we cannot say our lives are over, because God is not done with us yet. As one door is closing, God is opening the door to another plan. We must keep subjecting our moods to the promises of

Christ, not the pressures around us.

Be still: When the Psalmist was faced with diverse problems and difficulties, he came to a conclusion: *"Be still, and know that I am God: I will be exalted among the heathen, I will be exalted in the earth"* **(Psalms 46:10 KJV).** 'Being still' is one of the most difficult things for any human being. By nature, we are wired to move; to do things, to run around. But a time comes in our life when the only defense we can have against anxiety is to be still. One version said, "Let be and be still; know, recognize and understand that I am God." You may say that situation is terrible, but God is saying 'let it be...; know and understand that I am the Lord of this event.'

One day, I was about to go to the bank and I needed my driver's license for some transactions. I checked the safe where I usually keep it but could not find it. Rather than sit down to think of where it could be; I started searching for it. My wife joined in the search and we looked everywhere. In the process, I accidentally sat on my glasses and it got broken. Though I did not say anything, I felt very bad about the glasses. My wife noticed that I was not happy and tried to put my mind off it. She said, 'It is the glasses that got broken not your eyes.' But believe it

> God always has a process, He always has a pathway but His pathway is never revealed to an agitated mind; it will only come when you are restful.

or not, I couldn't listen to that sermon. I said to myself, 'why didn't the Lord show me where the driver's license was? Now in addition to not finding the driver's license, I had incurred another bill. As this feeling mounted, I went into my room. Then the word of the Lord came to me: 'Be still and know that I am God.' I decided to sit quietly before God. While in that stillness, the Lord revealed where the driver's license was and on that same day I got a completely free replacement for my glasses.

Can you see that we sometimes ignore God when faced with the stress of life? Even when the pains are too much to bear, we continue to ignore Him? Sometimes, all we need to have an answer is to still our soul. There are many problems that will arise to which we may never find a solution. Things will happen that you would not understand why they are happening. Rather than spending time worrying in such situations, be still and know that God is in charge. God always has a process, He always has a pathway but His pathway is never revealed to an agitated mind; it will only come when you are restful. Be still and know that I am God. God has a better solution on how to handle that crisis. There is a power in Christ that can make us overcome our moods. As a Christian, you can keep up with everyone. Why? Because of your union with Christ who infuses strength in you. When the situations become perplexing and the challenges overwhelming; that is the time to tell yourself, 'Be still and know that I am GOD.'

GET AWAY

Worry has gotten hold of several people because of their lack of rest. Rest goes a long way to soothe the nerves and clear the head. It gets you back in shape. I have discovered that everything looks better in the morning after a good night's sleep. Frequent breaks for relaxation keeps the tension down. Sometimes you need a holiday. Many of us work round the clock from Monday to Saturday; some even work on Sundays and we get so tensed up that we breakdown. 'Work-aholism' kills faster than alcoholism. Dr. John Haggai, the founder of the Haggai Institute of Advanced Leadership Training said,

"One of the best investments of discipline and effort you can make is in learning how to relax so that you can get proper rest, whether it be in full eight hours end to end or whether it be six hours with snoozes throughout the day, or whatever is the best for you." The Psalmists says: *"It is vain for you to rise up early, To sit up late, To eat the bread of sorrows; For so He gives His beloved sleep"* **(Psalms 127:2 NKJV)**. Relax, God is in control. He is overseeing your work and worries. Take a break, read a good novel, watch a good movie, listen to songs, talk to little children, take a stroll; get away from the tensed and highly pressurized environment. Go to the countryside and appreciate the vegetation. Take your mind off your anxieties.

In Matthew 6, Jesus directed our attention to nature. Look at the lilies of the garden, concentrate on their beauty for a while and you will be amazed at how peaceful and restful your heart can become. Move closer to nature and defuse your worries. Walter C. Hagen said, "Don't hurry, don't worry. You are only here for a short visit. So be sure to stop and smell the flowers." You may argue: 'I have several responsibilities. I simply have no time to play around. 'But could you be as busy as Jesus?' Have you ever heard that Jesus was tensed up and worried? Well, you might argue that Jesus has supernatural strength. However, Jesus was a man like you and he rested! **Mark 6:31-32** reads: *"And He said to them, (as for you) come away by yourselves to a deserted place and rest a while for many were (continually) coming and going and they had not even leisure enough to eat. And they went away in a boat to a solitary place by themselves'*. Perhaps you are one of those people Jesus was referring to in that passage "who had not even leisure enough to eat." As a song without a rhythm results in noise, so a life without frequent pauses end in chaos. Learn to relax. Do it your own way; you do not need to imitate someone else.

Many people have asked how I cope effectively with preaching, writing, working as a physician and being a husband and father at home. I thank God for His ever sufficient strength that has kept me this far but I also do my own part by taking frequent naps whenever the opportunity presents itself during the

> As a song without a rhythm results in noise, so a life without frequent pauses end in chaos.

day. It could be a few minutes but it gets me well rested enough to face the next task. Also, I go on holidays at least once in a year. This way, I am able to rest very well, review what has been done so far and seek God's face for the months or years ahead. Find your own way of relaxation. When your mind is getting bogged down with worries, defuse it. Someone said, 'When I feel worried and depressed, I simply remove my shoe, loosen my hair and start running. I lose myself in the wind. By the time, I have been running for an hour or so, I will be too spent to think'. Her way of defusing stress is running, yours could be something else. Get away from the hustle and bustle of your work place and find some place where you can relax. Martin Luther commented on what he usually does when he gets worried. He said, "When I am assailed with heavy tribulations I rush out among my pigs rather than remain alone by myself." The advice is very simple and straightforward: get away. May be you do not have pigs. But there are many other things that you can do to take yourself away from your troubles. Find it out and do it.

> "Life is too short to be little."
> - Benjamin Disraeli.

AIM HIGH

"Life is too short to be little," said Benjamin Disraeli. These words had a profound effect on Andre Morris who said in a magazine called 'This Week', "This statement has held me through many painful experiences." Often we allow small things to upset us when we should forget them. Dream big and make moves towards achieving them. You have to start aiming for the things that matter and stop getting hampered by little distractions. Dr Ben Carson, a renowned paediatric neurosurgeon at John Hopkins Hospital in Baltimore and the author of the book 'Think Big' wrote, "If you can learn to think big, nothing on earth will keep you from being successful in whatever you choose to do." How wide can you stretch your imagination and how high do you desire to get? Stretch it and you would get it. If you aim for the sky you might get to the tree top, if you aim for the tree-top you might get to the table-top, but if you aim for the table top you might never leave the ground.

Jesus emphasized His intention for us to aim high, when He was speaking in **Luke 12:31**, *"Only aim at and strive for and seek His kingdom and all these things shall be supplied to you also."* **(AMP)** The highest thing you can

> Obstacles bring out the potentials in you; the hidden capabilities.

aim is the kingdom of God. This is because it has, attached to it the strings of all the other goods of life. Many people are little because of what they seek. When you aim high, you become less concerned about the cause of your worry. Aiming high does not automatically wipe out the possibilities of problems. You will encounter problems on the way but how you handle them is what matters. Do you see your troubles as obstacles or as stepping-stones to your success? Joseph Sugarman said, "Each problem has hidden in it an opportunity so powerful that it literally dwarfs the problem. The greatest success stories were created by people who recognize a problem and turned it into an opportunity." On your way to achieving your aim, if you can turn every barrier to a stepping-stone, you will be successful.

Obstacles bring out the potentials in you; the hidden capabilities. A man of character attains greatness in difficult times, since it is only by coming to grips with difficulty that he

> Recognizing the fact that the 'raw material' in your hand is what is needed to make you great and maximizing it, is the key to success.

can recognize his potentials. How well are you prepared to meet the difficulties that might come your way? Are you the type that gives up and complain or are you ready to say to your dream, "Nothing can stop me from getting to you.' Aim high and use what you have in your hand. Use your God-given talents to achieve your goal. When you set your sight on high achievements, distractions are ignored. When you are doing the job at hand you would not be worried about things that do not matter. When you are focused, you would not succumb to distractions.

A goal worth reaching is not attained easily.

Several people complain of lack of opportunities. If you don't have opportunities, create one. Recognizing the fact that the 'raw material' in your hand is what is needed to make you great and maximizing it, is the key to success. Jonathan Winters said, "If your ship doesn't come in, swim out to it." Stop sitting in one place bemoaning your fate.

A goal worth reaching is not attained easily. So set out to achieve your aim. Aim high and frivolities would become little. Aim at God and your problems will become insignificant.

ENJOY THE PRESENCE OF GOD

An anointed atmosphere brings a serenity that is usually hard to explain. When the presence of God pervades an environment peace floods the heart and worry is banished. **Psalm 16:11** says, *"You will show me the path of life; in your presence is fullness of joy, at your right hand there are pleasures forevermore."* "Fullness of joy" indicates a state in which one's heart is overwhelmingly filled with so much joy that it displaces and dispels every trace of worry. God's presence has a way of overpowering and eliminating our worries.

There is this story of a man who was going through great trials. He was wrongly accused for a crime for which he was in no way responsible and this got him very worried. He fretted so much that he could not sleep. Then he developed shingles, an ailment caused by herpes infection, characterized by skin eruptions and accompanied by severe pain. He became very ill and got weaker every

> A Word-filled life will experience a worry-free existence.

day. Unfortunately, he did not let up on his worries and his condition worsened. It became so worse one night that he concluded he was not going to live to see the next day. Surprisingly, he woke up the next morning. He struggled down stairs and heard singing coming from the house chapel. The hymn floating towards him was 'God will take care of you.' Entering the chapel he sat down. At that instant, something inexplicable happened. He felt lifted from all his troubles and the peace of God flowed into him. From that day on, he regained his strength and freed himself from all his worries. The dramatic change in his life resulted from listening to that song: God will take care of you.

Perhaps your place of work is not near any church and you wonder: how can I get an anointed atmosphere? I have good news for you; you can create one! Listening to sermons or songs brings us into God's presence. Play them in your room and in your car. Surround yourself with the Word and Promises of God. Listen to the Audio Bible over and over again. Hearing the Word of God brings reassurance to our soul. It increases our faith and strengthens our hope. It fortifies us against our daily troubles and elevates us from the worries of life. Go for crusades and camp meetings. Go on a retreat. Mix with the people of God and get your anxiety over with. A Word-filled life will experience a worry-free existence.

CONQUER WORRY WITH HUMOUR AND LAUGHTER

To enjoy life, you have to learn humour. The day whose potential is least utilized is one in which there was no of laughter heard within its hours. Let there be laughter in the homes. Let there be joy at the workplace. Let there be dancing among the people. Laughter lightens the atmosphere, lessens the burden and helps you to let go of yourself. O. A. Battista, Canadian-American chemist and author, wrote, "Laugh at yourself and the rest of the world will laugh with you instead of at you." When you laugh at yourself, it does not mean that you think less of yourself. It just shows your ability to effectively handle unfavourable situations. Abraham Lincoln, during the difficult days of the civil war, said, "With the fearful strain that is on me night and day, if I did not laugh I should die."

The Director of Preventive Cardiology in University of Maryland, Baltimore, Dr. Miller, did a very important research, in which he compared one hundred and fifty people who have had heart disease with one hundred and fifty people who have never had heart disease. He assessed how they respond to life situations and to stress. His research showed that those who had heart problems were less likely to respond to stress with laughter. And those who looked at life situations with humour and joy were less likely to visit a cardiologist. Do you love your heart? Then have a good laugh.

Learn to laugh at yourself. Laughing will promote longevity, loosen you up and help you enjoy life. The Bible says that God laughs. **Psalm 2:4** records:

> **"In heaven the LORD laughs as he sits on his throne…" (CEV)**

If God could laugh, why would humans be antagonistic to laughter? Wilferd A. Peterson, renowned author of *The Art of Living*, wrote, "Laughter is the best medicine for a long and happy life. He who laughs last!" Laughter promotes well being, downplays our troubles and improves our relationships. Laughter is wholesome.

Proverbs 17:22 says,

"A merry heart does good like a medicine, but a broken spirit dries the bones."

The Good News Bible Translates that verse as:

"Being cheerful keeps you healthy. It is slow death to be gloomy all the time."

Arnold H. Glasow, American humorist said, "Laughter is a tranquilizer with no side effects." For good health, enjoyment of life, defeating life's challenges and possessing an internal control, we need a keen sense of humour and a good dose of mirth. The world has enough gloom without you adding to it. So learn to laugh. Ella Wheeler Wilcox, American author and poet, in her poem *Solitude* wrote, "Laugh and the world laughs with you, weep and you weep alone; for the sad old earth must borrow its mirth, but has trouble enough of its own." Humour declares man's superiority over the calamity that befalls him; it elevates us above life's misery. In reflection, Grenville Kleiser, North-American inspirational author, said, "Good humour is a tonic for the mind and body. It is the best antidote for anxiety and depression. It is a business asset. It attracts and keeps friends. It lightens human burdens. It is the direct route to serenity and contentment."

CAST YOUR CARES ON GOD

Throughout the book of Matthew 6:25, Jesus made us realise the power and loving kindness of a wonderful God. He brought to our realization the fact that God knows everything about us. He knows you need to eat, be educated, have good health and He cares. He is ready to provide all these and more. For God to know is for Him to care. God does not handle this knowledge passively, He acts on it. Worry can be effectively handled when you recognize that God knows. Jesus said, *"Are not two little sparrows sold for a penny? And yet not one of them will fall to the ground without your Father's leave (consent) and notice. But even the very hairs of your head are all numbered. Fear not then; you are of more value than many sparrows"* **(Matthew 10:29-31 AMP).** God has you in mind and when you acknowledge and accept this, your worries come to an end. Worry undermines God. **Proverb 3:5-6** says *"Never worry alone. Take it to the Lord and leave it there."* He is able to handle it. He doesn't need your help or assistance.

The Bible says in **Psalm 55:22**, *"Cast your burden on*

the Lord (releasing the weight of it) and He will sustain you; he will never allow the consistently righteous to be moved (made to slip, fall or fail)." He also repeated this instruction in **1 Peter 5:7**, *"Casting all your care upon Him, for He cares for you."* God is strong enough to handle all your worries, He is patient enough to understand you, He is rich enough to provide all your needs and cares enough to know you. Don't worry about tomorrow; God has got it under control. He is able to carry you through, just lean on him. **Philippians 4:19** says, *"And my God will liberally supply (fill to the full) your every need according to his riches in glory in Christ Jesus"* **(AMP).** His love can neither be qualified nor quantified. That was why he said in **Jeremiah 29:11**, *"For I know the thoughts and plans that I have for you, says the Lord, thoughts and plans for welfare and peace and not for evil, to give you hope in your final outcome."*

When you realize that God has many good things in store for you, then your worries becomes history. He says that he will not leave us desolate or comfortless, that though a mother could forget her sucking child yet He will not forget us. The Message Bible records: "Can a mother forget the infant at her breast, walk away from the baby she bore? But even if mothers forget, I'd never forget you--never. Look, I've written your names on the back of my hands. The walls you're rebuilding are never out of my sight" **(Isaiah 49:15-16).** God will never leave us alone.

Taking all our anxieties to this caring God, will free us from pains, burdens, body and heartaches. Take your problems to God in prayer. Acknowledge His power to help you overcome your difficulties. Maximise the fact that God has a listening ear. I always love listening to this old hymn, written by Joseph M. Scriven in 1855, because it reassures my heart:

> **What a Friend we have in Jesus**
> **All our sins and griefs to bear**
> **What a privilege to carry**
> **Everything to God in prayer**
> **Oh, what peace we often forfeit**
> **Oh what needless pains we bear**
> **All because we do not carry**
> **Everything to God in prayer.**

Oh! What needless diseases we bring upon ourselves, when we worry and do not take it to God. Oh! How miserable we have allowed our lives to become, just because of our lack of prayer. Why do we try to fight life battles alone when we can easily relinquish them to God? What a great mistake we make in worrying; it has no solution to our problems.

> "Casting the whole of your care (all your anxieties, all your worries all your concerns, once and for all) on Him, for He cares for you affectionately and cares about you watchfully." (AMP)

Off load your heart to God. He has enough space in His heart to handle your worries. Corrie Ten Boom wrote, "Never be afraid to trust an unknown future to a known God." Put everything into God's hand and trust His ability to take care of everything. Prayer is the greatest remedy for all the perplexities of life.

When you are not praying, you are worrying and when you are worrying, you become paralysed by the situations you worry about.

We cannot totally remove worry until we have replaced it with something better and that is prayer. Praying releases us from the bondage of worry. Give all your worries to God in prayer. He cares about you and is ready to take

> **Prayer is the greatest remedy for all the perplexities of life.**

your anxieties upon himself. Jesus has shown us by example that prayer brings relief to the soul. Are you a praying Christian? Or have you replaced prayer with worry in your life? When you are not praying, you are worrying and when you are worrying, you become paralysed by the situations you worry about. By praying we look beyond our situations and focus on God's infinite power; it indicates absolute trust in a loving Father. Reaching out to God in prayer, results in His reaching out to us in power.

He gives us power and strength to become conquerors. In prayer we surrender our troubles to God and we ask for divine assistance. David Hubbard said, "Our prayer expresses our commitment to Christ. By talking to God we affirm our basic decision to depend on Him." Praying to God about your problem is the best way of getting a solution. Why? God answers prayers! Bishop J.C. Ryle confirmed: "Prayer has obtained things that seemed impossible and out of reach. It has won victories over fire, air, earth and water. Prayer opened the Red Sea. Prayer brought water from the rock and bread from Heaven. Prayer made the sun stand still. Prayer brought fire from the sky on Elijah's sacrifice. Prayer overthrew the army of Sennacherib. Prayer has healed the sick. Prayer has raised the dead. Prayer has procured the conversion of countless souls."

Prayer is the key. It not only deals with the problem, it also eliminates worry from your life, and gives peace of mind.

> "**Don't worry about anything; instead pray about everything; tell God your needs and don't forget to thank Him for His answers. If you do this you will experience God's peace, which is far more wonderful than the human mind can understand. His peace will keep your thoughts and your hearts quiet and at rest as you trust in Christ Jesus" (Philippians 4:6-7 TLB).**

Friend, nothing lies beyond the power of on enduring prayer. Hannah prayed over her worries and got a historic son. The Bible records:

> "**So Hannah rose up after they had eaten in Shiloh, and after they had drunk. Now Eli the priest sat upon a seat by a post of the temple of the LORD. And she was in bitterness of soul, and prayed unto the LORD, and wept sore... And they rose up in the morning early, and**

worshipped before the LORD, and returned, and came to their house to Ramah: and Elkanah knew Hannah his wife; and the LORD remembered her. Wherefore it came to pass, when the time was come about after Hannah had conceived, that she bare a son, and called his name Samuel, saying, Because I have asked him of the LORD" (1 Samuel 1:9-10, 19-20 KJV).

Samuel eventually became one of the great prophets of Israel. Elijah prayed and there was no rain for three and a half years, he prayed again and heaven gave rain. The Apostle James reflected:

"Elijah was a man just like us, and he prayed earnestly for it not to rain, and it did not rain on the ground for three years and six months. Then he prayed again, and heaven sent rain, and the ground produced its crops" (James 5:17-18 ISV).

Hezekiah prayed and one hundred and eighty five thousand Assyrians fell in one night. He never lifted a sword.

"And Hezekiah prayed before the LORD, and said, O LORD God of Israel, which dwellest between the cherubims, thou art the God, even thou alone, of all the kingdoms of the earth; thou hast made heaven and earth... Now therefore, O LORD our God, I beseech thee, save thou us out of his hand, that all the kingdoms of the earth may know that thou art the LORD God, even thou only... And it came to pass that night, that the angel of the LORD went out, and smote in the camp of the Assyrians an hundred fourscore and five thousand: and when they arose early in the morning, behold, they were all dead corpses"** (2 Kings 19:15, 19, 35).

Are your problems bigger than you? Then, pray! Make prayer a part of your daily experience.

ABIDE IN CHRIST

What does it mean to abide in Christ? It is to rest in Him, wait on Him, depend in Him and rely on Him. When you abide in a person, you take on the character of the person, behave like the person and after a while portray his principles. Abiding in Christ is the most effective way of overcoming anxiety. God can be trusted. He can be depended on and when you abide in him, you have a sure rock of defense. Jesus said,

> "I am the vine; you are the branches. Whoever lives in me and I in him bears much (abundant) fruit. However, apart from me (cut off from vital union with me) you can do nothing" (John 15:5).

If you live in the true vine, Jesus Christ, then your life becomes a fulfilled and fruitful one. He said in **John 10:10**,

> "I came that they may have and enjoy life and have it in abundance (to the full, till it overflows)."

Jesus wants us to enjoy life. He does not want us to be miserable but this state of joyfulness is lacking in a worrier's life. What does it mean to abide in Christ?

It means *'concentrate on Christ'*. Look away from your troubles and look up to Christ. A person who is devoted to Christ and who hungers for him will not worry about things around him. Dr A.A. Brill, a psychiatrist, said, "Anyone who is truly religious does not develop a neurosis." Take time to talk to Jesus, make him your focus. *"Looking unto Jesus, the author and finisher of our faith"* (Hebrews 12:2). In looking up to Jesus, you would be able to emulate his character and learn how he handles things.

To abide in Christ means to *'maintain a strong confidence'* in the midst of the vicissitudes of life. Believe that God has a plan for your future. Paul said in **Philippians 1:6**,

> **"Being confident of this very thing that He which hath begun a good work in you will perform it until the day of Jesus Christ."**

Are you courageous enough to withstand the circumstances of life? Can you confidently proclaim the verse above? David said,

> **"The LORD is my light and my salvation; whom shall I fear? The LORD is the strength of my life; of whom shall I be afraid?" (Psalms 27:1 KJV).**

Is your faith in God strong enough to make you confident in Him? **Jeremiah 29:11** says:

> **"For I know the thoughts and plans that I have for you says the Lord, thoughts and plans for welfare and peace and not for evil, to give you hope in your final outcome" (AMP).**

I like the word 'your final outcome.' God has a wonderful plan for us, which will take time to mature. Before that final outcome, there could be storms; nevertheless if we abide and have confidence in Him, the end will be glorious. The past and the present are stages in the plan of God, which combine together in the future to project the glorious display of God's intention in the 'final outcome'. Believe that God is going to give you a future and he will do it! Never doubt the power of God to turn your life around and make your future great.

> God is an anchor that never breaks under the weight of all the waves, storms and problems of our lives.

Abiding in Christ means *'using God as a strong anchor.'* The Hebrew writer said in 6:19, *"Now we have this hope as a sure and steadfast anchor of the soul (it cannot slip and it cannot break down under whoever steps out upon it a hope) that reaches farther and enters into the very certainty of the Presence within the veil."* God is an anchor that never breaks under the weight of all the waves, storms and vicissitudes of our lives. If we lay it upon Him, we will be able to stand unshaken and will not be tossed about with the storms of life. Are you abiding in Christ? A life outside Christ is a life in crisis.

There comes a time in the life of everyman when he

realizes the fact that money is transient, that sex is a passing pleasure, that properties soon vanish but that only God is permanent in life. Give Christ a place in your heart and enjoy peace in His presence.

CHAPTER six

TRUST: THE VICTORY OVER WORRY

> Trusting God is the key to overcoming life's problems.
> **Greg Erhabor**

A verse that has continually stirred me is found in Proverbs 3: 5: "Trust in the LORD with all your heart, and lean not on your own understanding." The biblical meaning of the word 'trust' derived from the original Greek word, *'pisteuo'* which means 'to have confidence in, have faith in, entrust, especially one's spiritual well-being to Christ, to believe in, to commit and put in trust with.' When the scripture says 'trust the Lord,' it means feel safe, feel secure; it means stop worrying about your life because God cares about you. In explaining what trust is, one bible commentator said, "...This type of hope is a constant expectation, no matter what is happening. It's a hope that knows no limit; not a constant anxiety, it's a constant expectation."

> If you must conquer worry, you must go
>
> If you must conquer worry, you must go beyond the voices of men around you or voices within you and try to find the voice of God.

All through his teachings, we see Jesus trying to tell us that in life, we have two options: to be anxious, worried and not trust Him or to just trust Him and not be anxious or worried. It has been said, "The beginning of trust is the end of anxiety and the end of anxiety is the beginning of trust. But the end of trust is the beginning of anxiety." You can't trust and be anxious. Solomon told his son,

> "Trust GOD from the bottom of your heart; don't try to figure out everything on your own. Listen for GOD's voice in everything you do, everywhere you go; he's the one who will keep

you on track. Don't assume that you know it all. Run to GOD! Run from evil!" (Proverbs 3:5-7 The MSG).

Don't try to figure everything out on your own out, listen to God's voice. When we are in a state of anxiety and worry about things; we get confused by background noises. The ability to tune in to hear God gets blurred. If you must conquer worry, you must go beyond the voices of men around you or voices within you and try to find the voice of God. Regardless of what we go through, or the pains we meet in life, when we seek well enough, we will find the voice of God. We would discover that to every situation, there is a divine challenge. This was what Habakkuk did,

> "I will stand upon my watch, and set me upon the tower, and will watch to see what he will say unto me..." (Habakkuk 2:1 KJV).

When David was worried about how the wicked were prospering, he waited on the Lord and He ministered to him.

> "But as for me, my feet were almost gone; my steps had well nigh slipped. For I was envious at

the foolish; when I saw the prosperity of the wicked. For there are no bands in their death: but their strength is firm. They are not in trouble as other men; neither are they plagued like other men...When I thought to know this, it was too painful for me; Until I went into the sanctuary of God; then understood I their end. Surely thou didst set them in slippery places: thou castedst them down into destruction" (Psalms 73:2-5, 16-18 KJV).

If there is anything I want to do in this book, it is to convince you to leave worry alone and trust God. David said,

"I have been young, and now am old; yet have I not seen the righteous forsaken, nor his seed begging bread." (Psalms 37:25 KJV)

This is the testimony of a man whose life was full stress. He was a fugitive who lived most of his early life running from King Saul. There were times his life was in jeopardy. In spite of all the difficulties David went through, he could see the hand of God in his desert, in the loneliness of his life; in the frustrations he went through and he could testify of God's goodness. He further said, "Oh, taste and see that the LORD is good; blessed is the man who trusts in Him!" **(Psalms 34:8 NKJV)**

Very often these days, we hear one preacher or the other assuring us of wonderful things if we can only trust God. When we trust God based on earthly rewards, we often get disappointed and may lose faith in God's control of our lives. Trusting in God does not mean we would not face life's troubles. Jesus said, "These things I have spoken to you, that in me you may have peace. In the world you will have tribulation; but be of good cheer, I have overcome the world." **(John 16:33 NKJV)** Trust gives us peace in the midst of troubles and hope when all is lost.

God has the Master Plan

Many of us are trying to manipulate things. We calculate and try to figure out things in our heads. We contemplate that if God promises us something, then this must be the way He will do it. However, I want you to know that this is not how God works; our projections are far from His.

Isaiah 55:8-9 says,

> "I don't think the way you think. The way you

work isn't the way I work, GOD's Decree. For as the sky soars high above earth, so the way I work surpasses the way you work, and the way I think is beyond the way you think" (The MSG).

In trusting God, you should realize one thing; it is only God that has the master plan. Regardless of how much you and I try to figure God out, He alone holds the blueprint. The Bible says,

> **"That's why we have this Scripture text: No one's ever seen or heard anything like this, Never so much as imagined anything quite like it-- What God has arranged for those who love him" (1 Corinthians 2:9 The MSG).**

The scriptures said about the life of our Lord Jesus Christ:

> **"But we speak the wisdom of God in a mystery, even the hidden wisdom, which God ordained before the world unto our glory. Which none of the princes of this world knew: for had they known it, they would not have crucified the Lord of glory" (1 Corinthians 2:7-8).**

Can you imagine Satan with all his supposed powers yet he could not unravel the plan of God? Some of us waste our time going to prophets, soothsayers, clairvoyants and palm readers to figure out our future but the Bible says that 'what God had planned, demons do not know.'

If you are going to stop worrying, you must believe that God has the master plan and if it seems that the plan 'A' has not worked for you, don't forget that He always has a plan 'B'. God will not allow you to miss out on the fun of youth, he will not make you miss out on the joy of fatherhood or the joy of motherhood; he will not let you miss out on the goodness of this life. After all, the scripture says, God *"...has given us richly all things to enjoy"* **(1 Timothy 6:17)**.

He is so concerned about us and He is saying 'Son, daughter, listen to me. Don't get worried; I am involved in your life, I am involved in your reproach, I am involved in your adversity. I am right there with you, we are partners in this business. Don't think you are alone, don't try to figure things out. I have my plans and I just want you to trust me. Just trust and believe me, you will not miss out on anything.' If God says we should trust him and we will not miss out on anything then I think we should just trust Him.

God works Miracles

God's method is unpredictable. There has been no one in scripture or living who can predict God. No one can say 'surely this is the way God will work.' In fact, God has the power and the ability to use things that you don't consider of worth and adorn such things with worth. Those things that you think are useless, God can make such things majestic.

> "Jesus saith unto them, Did ye never read in the scriptures, The stone which the builders rejected, the same is become the head of the corner: this is the Lord's doing, and it is marvellous in our eyes?" (Matthew 21:42 KJV)

Though rejected, God made that stone the most significant thing. The reason is - He is a God of miracles. If you say you trust God, you must believe in miracles. If it will take a miracle to turn your situation around, then for your sake, He will do it. If it will take miracles for you to progress, believe He will do it. God is involved, God is concerned, He cares and He does miracles, just believe him.

> The scriptures did not say 'under His wings shall thou see but under his wings shall thou trust.'

I know someone might say, 'I am facing the dark moments of life and it seems God is not answering my prayers. I have believed God for certain things but have not gotten them.' I want you to know that God still works miracles. You need to believe Him.

There was the story of a man who was distressed that God was not answering his prayers. On listening to a sermon on trust, he remarked, "I find it difficult to trust Him when He is not in sight." Somebody replied him, "If you can trust somebody only when you see him, then you don't trust him." 2 Corinthians 5:7 says, "For we walk by faith, not by sight." As they were talking, they saw a chick being covered by the mother hen. The brother asked the worried Christian, 'Can that chick see afar off?' He said 'No.' 'What can it see?' 'It can only see the wing of her mother covering it.' Then the brother told this man, 'The Psalmist says, "He shall cover thee with his feathers, and under his wings shalt thou trust: his truth *shall be thy* shield and buckler"

> The highest expression of our faith is not trusting God for unceasing blessings but absolute trust in God in unpredictable circumstances.

(Psalms 91:4). The scriptures did not say 'under his wings shall thou see but under his wings shall thou trust.'

Corrie Ten Boom, was a Jewish Christian lady, who suffered a lot in the Nazi camp. God delivered her and towards the end of her life she wrote, "Never be afraid to trust an unknown future to a known God." If all that remains in life is God, He is enough. God is enough to turn your situations around and meet your needs.

Don't be Mad at God

You don't need to worry about your circumstances. Stop being mad at God, He is at work on your behalf. Maybe there is someone who tells you, I trusted God for promotion, yet I am at the bottom rung. Friend, that is a poison you must not swallow. That person wants to stand between you and God. Hold on to the word of God and trust Him. All through history, everyone that has trusted God implicitly had seen the hands of God.

> Trust the past to God's mercy, the present to his love and the future to his providence.

The highest expression of our faith is not trusting God for unceasing blessings but absolute trust in God in unpredictable circumstances. You don't show you trust God when everything seems to be fine but your trust is put to test when things are not going as planned. That is what it means to trust God. Paul wrote the Romans:

> "**Trusting means looking forward to getting something we don't yet have; for a man who already has something doesn't need to hope that he will get it**" **(Romans 8:24 Living Bible).**

Trusting God simply means that we believe God is going to give us the things we need. Keep on believing that God has a better idea, that God has a better plan. Though the situation may look dark, God can weave out of our dark yesterdays, a glorious tomorrow. Out of the life that has been so miserable, God can draft out a beautiful symphony.

Don't take Panic Measures

Some people don't trust God enough, so they tend to run ahead of Him. Isaac Watts wrote: "O Lord our help in ages past, our hope for years to come, be thou our guide while trouble last and our eternal hope." Someone wrote, "Trust the past to God's mercy, the present to his love and the future to his providence."

Trusting God means holding onto God in spite of the fact that things are not working right, it may mean living from hand to mouth. It seems to me that sometimes when we trust God, He might not give us certain provisions in excess but God always has his miraculous moments. He wants us to follow him every step of the way.

You may say 'God I want you to help me build a house but I don't have all the blocks needed for the house.' But He says, 'Just trust me to get one block for today.' Don't worry about how you will get all the blocks but trust God for one block at a time. That is why Jesus says, *"...Sufficient for the day is its own trouble."* (Matthew 6:34) Those who learn to trust and believe God know that sometimes, they may have to live from hand to mouth.

I remember when we were building our church, during the early days of the ministry. The church complex was costing millions of naira and we were a young congregation with most of us being civil servants and students. Sometimes I wondered where the next money will come from. I got to know that this is God's work and I am only a channel. The moment I laid everything at Jesus' feet, it made a tremendous difference. Within a few years we completed the complex debt free. God sometimes brings us to situations when we can look to no other source than to trust Him. I believe that God always answers at the right time.

Change your old Mindset

Many of us have our minds set in a particular manner; we have an idea of how we think things should work. You believe God for a breakthrough and you suppose it will come when you travel abroad. You are trusting God for a particular favour but you believe it has to come through a certain uncle. Trusting God may require you to change your mind set. God does not work according to our scheming.

Don't have a fixed mind set. Certain times the enemy will give you offers that looks very good but behind those offers are traps of destruction. You must wean yourself from materialistic mindsets. God doesn't need things to bless you, He only needs His Person. He told Abram,

"...I *am* thy shield, *and* thy exceeding great reward" **(Genesis 15:1).** Don't worry about possessions; I am sufficient for you. "But seek ye first the kingdom of God, and his righteousness; and all these things shall be added unto you" **(Matthew 6:33).**

Why not trust the Lord during the dark periods of life, through your pains and your struggles. Perhaps, God has not granted your requests, because He wants to get your attention. He may be delaying because there is something in your life you have not addressed; there may be an attitude you have not taken time to address. Perhaps you are not ripe for the promotion you are asking for; the Bible says "the prosperity of fools shall destroy them." Don't be in haste, learn to trust God.

I met a young lady sometimes ago, who had been trusting God for a spouse. The lady was very active in the church and very good in leading prayers but her attitude was unpleasant. I told her although you are trusting God to give you a husband, men would tolerate you at a prayer meeting but will find it difficult to stay with you at home. God was delaying her in other to get her attention. She had an attitude problem she had to address. Trusting

God does not exonerate you from being responsible and responsive to His voice. Your faith must be substantiated by good works.

I don't know why you are having delays but periods like these give you the opportunity to search yourself. What is God trying to get at? What do you need to change? What is God pointing at in our personal lives or in our ministries? God wants to build your character before giving you the 'calling.' You will get wealth but God wants to prepare you first. Popularity is easy to come by but character takes years to develop. What is God drawing your attention to? God is not a magician. He wants to build character in us. He wants us to be people of competence, of vast resources, people who have mastered life and have put things under control. God doesn't just want to give us one shot at His glory. He wants us to abide in it.

Learn to trust God, learn to take Him a day at a time. You may be living from hand to mouth today but believe it; your moment of miracle will come because God has the master plan. God has everything under control, even in the depths of our sorrow or at the height of our afflictions, we can still trust God. We can say like Job, *"Though he slay me, yet will I trust in him"* **(Job 13:15)** *and know that "Though your beginning was small, yet your latter end would increase abundantly"* **(Job 8:7).**

CHAPTER SEVEN

TAKING CAPTIVE OF YOUR THOUGHTS AND IMAGINATIONS

> The mind grows by what it feeds on.
> **Holland**

What determines if a person will have a happy, joyful personality or be a constant worrier is not dependent on external factors, what somebody did or did not do; it is dependent on something on the inside- his thoughts and imaginations. Our thoughts rule our world.

Matthew 6:31 says,

"Therefore take no thought saying."

Can you see the relationship between what we think and what we say? For you to control what you say or what you do, you must first control the way you think. Jesus was indirectly saying that when you take a thought and you say it, invariably what you say becomes established. Paul wrote in the book of **2 Corinthians 10:3-5**,

> "For though we walk in the flesh, we do not war after the flesh: For the weapons of our warfare are not carnal, but mighty through God to the pulling down of strong holds; Casting down imaginations, and every high thing that exalteth itself against the knowledge of God, and bringing into captivity every thought to the obedience of Christ."

The New International Version translates it more explicitly,

> "For the weapon of our warfare are not of the flesh but divinely powerful for the destruction of fortresses, we are destroying speculations and every lofty thing raised up against the

knowledge of God and we are taking every thought captive to the obedience of Christ."

I don't know what goes through your mind but these thoughts are what determine the eventual outcome of your life. Our thoughts reflect the state of our inner chambers; they reside in the sanctuary of our minds. They are the building blocks of our internal fortress and mold our personality externally. Every sixty seconds in a minute and for every sixty minutes in an hour, our mind is undergoing an internal dialogue with us. Every now and then, we are talking to ourselves through the medium and avenue of our thoughts. What determines whether you will be an anxious person or a person who has power over worry is your control over that internal dialogue.

> Your thoughts today will determine what you will be tomorrow and what you are today is what you have thought yesterday.

The devil has his greatest grip in the mind. What we call evil, vices, worry, or bitterness all arise from the suggestion that he puts into our mind. We were never told whether Satan appeared physically to tempt Jesus but I believe the temptation took place in the battlefield of the mind. Satan brought suggestions and insinuations, he brought speculations and lofty thoughts to Christ's mind, but Jesus decided in the internal dialogue to put a stop to Satan and He replied Satan based on the Word of God.

> Our actions are trying to catch up with our thoughts.

Your thoughts make or mar you

Nothing makes a man have self-pity, self-doubt, self-deprecation quicker than the kind of thoughts he puts into his mind. When you see someone who is easily disturbed, who does not have the courage to face circumstances or who feels that the whole world is against him, know that somewhere inside his mind, he has lost the battle.

Our thoughts could be snares, which we fall into and are trapped, they could be thieves that rob us of the great things that God has given us, they could enslave us but they could also liberate us. That was why Paul said we should learn to bring our thoughts into captivity. This means our thoughts should be restrained and confined. It should be made to be obedient; and subjected to the

TAKING CAPTIVE OF YOUR THOUGHTS AND IMAGINATIONS

teaching and the principles of God.

Your thoughts today will determine what you will be tomorrow and what you are today is what you have thought yesterday. Our actions are trying to catch up with our thoughts. I have met people who told me, I thought it will happen and it really happened. I have counseled women who said, 'I know my husband will leave me' and truly the man leaves them. Someone said, "When you sow a thought, you reap an action; when you sow an action, you reap a habit. When you sow a habit and you reap a character; when you sow a character, you reap a lifestyle. When you sow a lifestyle, you reap a destiny." If only you can bring those thoughts, dreams, imaginations, speculations and insinuations into captivity, then you will be triumphant. By giving your thought a swing, you allow it to take control of you, to be in charge of your life and by doing so you fail.

If you have a well structured house, and desire to make it very beautiful, you will determine the kind of furniture you will put in that house. If you want this house to be a great edifice, you will be selective of the kind of furniture you bring into this house. So it is with our thoughts. Our thoughts are in our inner fortress, our internal sanctuary and God has given us the power and the control to decide the kind of thoughts we bring into our minds. When we see things we do not want to be part of our minds, then it is our right and our duty to remove those things from our minds.

Proverb 4:23 says,

> "Keep your heart with all diligence, for out of it spring the issues of life" (NKJV).

The Good News Bible translates,

> "Be careful how you think; your life is shaped by your thoughts."

Jesus says,

> "Do you not yet understand that whatever enters the mouth goes into the stomach and is eliminated? But those things which proceed out of the mouth come from the heart, and they defile a man. For out of the heart proceed evil thoughts, murders, adulteries, fornications, thefts, false witness, blasphemies. These are the things which defile a man..." (Matthew 15: 17-20).

Indirectly Jesus was saying, when you give words to your thoughts, you make those thoughts formidable and established and it is those things that invariably defiles you. So the defilement process starts from within; it does not come from without. Jesus said,

> "...If therefore the light that is in you is darkness, how great is that darkness!" (Matthew 6:23).

There is only one thing that you have absolute control over, which if you abdicate the responsibility to another person you will never be a happy person, and that is your thoughts. You must determine to exercise control over the things that proceed out of you; over the things that come out of your being. The greatest revolution that happened to me as a young Christian occurred when I read in **Proverbs 23:7,** *"For as he thinks in his heart, so is he."* That verse turned my life round. To me it means that regardless of what my boss thinks about me, or what my friends think about me, or what the society thinks about me, none of these people have the right to determine who I am.

It is your 'in-look' that will determine your outlook.

What will determine the kind of person I am or the person I will become is the kind of thoughts I have about myself. If the thoughts I have about myself are that of low self-esteem, a thousand and one people saying that I am great cannot mend it. If inside my being, I feel I am not loved, pouring all the love in this world on me can never turn the situation around. If I believe that I can never make it in life, no matter the encouragement people give me, I will resist it because I have shaped my life by my thoughts. I want to encourage you today, that the greatest battle will be fought not outside you but inside you. It is your 'in-look' that will determine your outlook.

Choose to think differently

I have seen people say about a particular man: he is such a nice man, he is such a wonderful person. Those around him commend him. Then I see this same person go into another setting and somebody says he is such a wicked person. I begin to ask myself, 'How can people say he is very good in this place and in another situation, he is regarded as being very bad?' Then I concluded, 'It is not so much that this man is bad or that he is good. It is the different perceptions people have of his personality based on their experiences with him. And if they decide to put good thoughts into their minds about him, then to them, he will be a good person.'

Jesus chose to think differently. He chose to embrace good thoughts and see things in the right perspective and he lived a worry-free life because of that. When the spies were sent out by Moses to go and scout the Promised Land, these people actually gave a direct description of what they saw. Truly those people were giants in comparison to them but God did not want them to speak and see through the physical eyes. He wanted them to see things with the eyes of the spirit. In their minds they assessed their situation and summarized their abilities:

> **"And there we saw the giants, the sons of Anak, which come of the giants: and we were in our own sight as grasshoppers, and so we were in their sight" (Numbers 13:33).**

Because of this, they never entered into the land God promised them. We are consistently insinuating, speculating and making deductions from the eyes of the flesh but God wants us to move higher. If we have to overcome the habit of worry, we have to rise to a higher level in our thinking.

David's victory over Goliath did not happen when he slung the stone to hit Goliath. Long before he met Goliath, David has defeated him in his mind. He said, *"For who is this uncircumcised Philistine, that he should defy the armies of the living God?"* **(1 Samuel 17:26)**. In his mind's eye, he equated him to the bear and lion that came to take his father's sheep. The battle was already won in the battlefield of the mind and the physical battle was just a demonstration. This was reflected in David's boldness as he walked to meet Goliath,

> **"…You come to me with a sword, with a spear, and with a javelin. But I come to you in the name of the LORD of hosts, the God of the armies of Israel, whom you have defied. This day the LORD will deliver you into my hand, and I will strike you and take your head from you. And this day I will give the carcasses of the camp of the Philistines to the birds of the air and the wild beasts of the earth, that all the earth may know that there is a God in Israel. Then all this assembly shall know that the**

LORD does not save with sword and spear; for the battle is the LORD'S, and He will give you into our hands" (1 Samuel 17: 45-47).

David was a man who had conquered his thoughts in his mind. Long before the battle, his spirit had continually communed with God and he had brought his thoughts to submit to the power of God. He declared,

> O LORD of hosts, blessed is the man that trusteth in thee." (Psalm 84:12)

> "The LORD is my shepherd; I shall not want" (Psalm 23:1).

> "The LORD taketh my part with them that help me: therefore shall I see my desire upon them that hate me" (Psalms 118:7).

He has been rehearsing these things from time to time in his spirit so much so that when he met Goliath, the victory had already been won. Things are twice created; first in the inner chamber of your being and then in the public arena of life. Begin to think thoughts that can benefit your life. Think prosperity, think goodness, think righteousness, think victory, think joy, think self-control.

What you say will stay.

Never permit evil thoughts to flow through your mouth

Jesus says *'take no thought saying'* because the relationship between our thoughts and our words are inseparable. Sometimes when all sorts of thoughts pass through our minds and the only way of making sure that those thoughts do not get established is not to allow it flow through our mouth. A thousand and one suggestions can come to our minds, but we must be ready to close our mouths against them and say, 'No, I will not permit these thoughts to be established with my mouth.'

> If you say you cannot, you will not; if you say you can, you will.

Don't allow the devil use your 'mouth' to announce his plans and wishes. The Christian does not cling to 'reality' but to 'revelation;' not to facts but to faith. The wise King Solomon says,

> "Death and life are in the power of the tongue: and they that love it shall eat the fruit thereof" (Proverbs 18:21 KJV).

The words you speak establish the life you live. What you say will stay. Never develop a steady conduit between your mind and mouth. Learn to have a stop gap, a check point where all thoughts can be thoroughly assessed. Mount a garrison between your mind and your mouth. Do not say what you don't want to happen. Don't establish wrong things with your mouth. The Bible says in **Romans 10:10**,

> "For with the heart man believeth unto righteousness; and with the mouth confession is made unto salvation."

If you say you cannot, you will not; if you say you can, you will. Whatsoever you say become yours. It is what you say that becomes established. How your life will turn out starts in the inner chambers of your being. It starts from believing the fact that 'because my life is controlled by my thoughts I will decide to choose my thoughts and my words. I will not give anyone the right to choose my thought for me.'

Bathe your mind with God's Words

I don't know what you say to your mind every now and then. I noticed that regardless of how much I bathe my body in the morning, by the time I am removing my shirt in the evening, there are usually stains on it. In a sense, no matter how well we scrub our bodies; there will still be dirt on it. We have to keep cleaning our body every day. If we can spend such time diligently washing our bodies every day, then we should spend more time with our minds. Paul told the Romans,

> **"And do not be conformed to this world, but be transformed by the renewing of your mind, that you may prove what is that good and acceptable and perfect will of God" (Romans 12:2 NKJV).**

Our minds are cleansed by washing with the Word of God on a daily basis. We make ourselves pure by using the word of God as a spiritual soap and water to cleanse our minds. The mind is the battlefield between good and evil, success and failure, significance and mediocrity - that is where the battle takes place. To be victorious you have to use the artillery of the Word of God.

The Word is able to counter any evil thought that passes through your mind. **Hebrews 4:12** says, *"For the word of God is quick, and powerful, and sharper than any two-edged sword, piercing even to the dividing asunder of soul and spirit, and of the joints and marrow, and is a* *discerner of the thoughts and intents of the heart"* **(KJV)**. Jesus did not overcome temptation by fighting with the devil; he simply used the Word of God. *"And when the tempter came to Him, he said, If You are the Son of God, command that these stones be made bread. But He answered and said, It is written, 'Man shall not live by bread alone, but by every word that proceeds out of the mouth of God"* **(Matthew 4:3-4)**. Jesus studied the word, he knew the word and when problems arose, he was able to use the word.

I want to encourage you to daily bathe your mind with the Word of God. Read the Bible, study the Word, meditate on the Word, imbibe the Word and above all use the Word to conquer in the battlefield of the mind. You will face challenges at work but what will determine your victory over those challenges will be how well you have conquered your mind. It does not matter what people say about you, your friends may say you are not doing well. It is not what people say that matters; it is what you think you are that you are! And this image of you is better shaped by the Word of God.

You mind set will determine your response to situations and this will determine how your life will turn out. Our lives are like trains moving in a certain direction and the baggage of those trains are the kinds of things we put in our minds. Whether this train will arrive at its destination or not, depend a lot on the people and baggages we decide to put on or remove from our trains. A legion of demons saying we are evil does not make us evil, and a host of angels shouting we are good, does not make us good, it is our thoughts and words that will determine our destiny.

Say and think good thoughts about yourself

One of the things we learnt in human psychology is that we have the ability to suggest things to our minds. In fact, a section of human psychology emphasizes what is called 'autosuggestion'- being able to convince ourselves of the true fact, by space repetition. Begin to think and say good thoughts about yourself and your life will begin to respond to what you say. Jesus said,

> **"And you shall know the truth, and the truth shall make you free" (John 8:32 MKJV).**

The truth is supposed to set us free but our thoughts sometimes put us in bondage and confine us to captivity. Will you allow your thoughts rob you of God's glory? Will you allow worries overtake you? Maybe you will need to meditate on the fact that *"your heavenly father knows."* Your heavenly Father knows you need a car, he knows you need a job; he knows you need a spouse, He knows your need food. And Christ assured us that He will provide. Let your mind begin to believe that your heavenly father knows and cares. When thoughts come into your mind to remind you that you are an orphan with no sponsor, remind yourself that your heavenly Father knows.

Remind yourself that *"every good gift and every perfect gift is from above and comes down from the Father of lights, with whom is no variableness nor shadow of turning"* **(James 1:17)**. Remind yourself that every issue of life till death is determined by your heavenly Father. *"He that is our God is the God of salvation and unto GOD the Lord belong the issues from death"* **(Psalms 68:20)**. Be reminded that promotion is not the work of a great boss or a great connection. *"For promotion cometh neither from the east, nor from the west, nor from the south; but God is the judge: he putteth down one, and setteth up another"* **(Psalms 75:6-7 KJV)**. Remind yourself that not even a sparrow will fall without your heavenly Father taking note; *"Are not five sparrows sold for two farthings, and not one of them is forgotten before God? But even the very hairs of your head are all numbered. Fear not therefore: ye are of more value than many sparrows"* **(Luke 12:6-7)**.

Flood your mind with good thoughts, reject worry and anxiety, embrace the beauty of life in your inner man. Have you sinned and failed again, facing the accuser's torment, remind yourself that God has not finished with you yet. When the enemy accuses you and says, 'For you, Christianity is impossible, it is not for sinners like you. You are trapped in lust and ensnared by your wrong behaviour. Here you go - the talkative and cantankerous person. Here you go - the filthy person. Here you go - the rejected person.' Remind him that *"...He who has begun a good work in you will complete it until the day of Jesus Christ"* **(Philippians 1:6 NKJV)**. Also remind him that *"there is therefore now no condemnation to them which are in Christ Jesus, who walk not after the flesh, but after the Spirit"* **(Romans 8:1)**.

When Jesus met the adulterous woman, he made one great statement. He said to her, *"...Neither do I condemn you; go and sin no more"* **(John 8:11)**. Sometimes our minds condemn us, but remind your mind that failures are potholes on the high road to success. A great statesman said: "Success is going from one failure to another without losing your optimism." The reason is that the broken pieces of our failure are elements God will use to build a formidable life. So remind yourself of that. Sometimes you will need to tell the enemy that the past is past. If you don't bury your past, it will bury you. Tell yourself that the train has passed that station and God is the future focus. God does not look back and that is why He says,

> "For I know the plans I have for you, says the Lord. They are plans for good and not for disaster, to give you a future and a hope" (Jeremiah 29:11 NLT).

In **Isaiah 43:18-19**, He says,

> "Remember ye not the former things, neither consider the things of old. Behold, I will do a new thing; now it shall spring forth; shall ye not know it? I will even make a way in the wilderness, *and* rivers in the desert."

Don't build a tabernacle around the past. Don't dwell on

the mistakes of the past. The train of life does not stop in just one station; the train is on the move. If you have never had a past, you will not know that God can forgive you. The past has no power over the future because God says, *"For I will be merciful to their unrighteousness, and their sins and their iniquities will I remember no more"* **(Hebrews 8:12).**

To overcome the root and habit of worry, we need to consistently remind ourselves of these things. We need to remind ourselves that God is for us. God is for you. What can you exchange for the blessed presence of the Holy Ghost? Nothing shall separate you from the love of God. These words were written several years ago and they antedate every sin or mistake you can ever make. God saw your future and made provisions before you were created.

> Victory in the war within determines victory without. Never go through the world armed with low self-esteem.

Consistently fill your mind with those thoughts; allow those good thoughts to govern your mind.

Tell yourself God is faithful and that you are fearfully and wonderfully made. Don't bother saying; 'if only I was a little bit handsome, if only I was prettier, if only I was more intelligent if only I was better shaped,' you are fearfully and wonderfully made. Don't be apologetic for the way you were created, you owe no man no apology for your looks. God specially constructed you. That is where the seed of worry must be destroyed. Are you going to go to your husband's house, expecting him to make you happy or feel better about yourself? I am sorry that is a dream that may never be fulfilled. Are you running home, expecting your father to comfort you? It may be a mirage that never materializes. There is a victory we have in Jesus, this is the victory that overcomes the world. The world around us is a battle ground but victory in the war within determines victory without. Never go through the world armed with a low self-esteem, don't go through the life battered and defeated in your mind. Take authority over your thoughts and win through life.

CHAPTER EIGHT

WHEN THERE SEEMS TO BE A DELAY

> Delay is not denial.
> **Anon**

No one worries more than the person, who believes that there is a delay in his life. When things are happening latter than expected, when major events of life are slowing down for them, when they look at their peers and they do not measure up, they begin to wonder 'why this delay?'

Delay may take various forms. Many people who are successful in their careers and in every other thing find themselves plodding through life alone. A lot of people are leaders in their corporate institutions, have houses and cars, can easily afford holidays out of the country but have no one to share their lives with. They have everything that they need to get that spouse but it doesn't just seem to happen. The delay may be that of having a child. You have been declared medically fit; no blocked tubes, no hormone imbalance, no history of past infections or abortions, sound womb, great body but no child. You have believed and trusted God, yet there is a delay. It may be a promotion or a job. It may be the simple things of life; financial breakthrough, becoming debt-free, getting another car or house but it seems there is a delay and you are not getting the things you have asked God to give you.

To some, the delay may be a spiritual desire in which you believe God to raise you to greater spiritual heights but every time you discover that you have not gotten there, there is a delay. Sometimes the delay may be that we are slow in getting the things God has promised us. Perhaps God has promised that He will improve your life in one dimension or the other. Rather than getting these promises, you observe that things are not happening the way you expect them, you are not catching up, things are getting postponed.

Jesus addressed this crucial issue in **Matthew 6:31-32**,

> "**Therefore do not worry, saying, 'What shall we eat?' or 'What shall we drink?' or 'What shall we wear?' For after all these things the Gentiles seek. For your heavenly Father knows that you need all these things.**"

Here Jesus was saying that you have got no cause to be anxious, there is no reason to worry, fume or fret. The key lies in the contrast between you and the Gentiles. Gentile here means the people who do not know God, who do not know His son, Jesus; who have not been redeemed - the unbelievers. Jesus was making us recognize that you and I are the sons and daughters of God. So when next you begin to say 'what will I eat' or 'what will I wear?', then you are reasoning and thinking like the Gentiles.

All that gives a Gentile pride are his material possessions. What he has achieved by personal prowess. But the Bible is saying you are not supposed to be like that. The reason is 'you are the son or daughter of God.' You are special to him.

> "But ye are a chosen generation, a royal priesthood, an holy nation, a peculiar people" (1 Peter 2:9 KJV).

God has particularly summoned you. The word 'call' means that God has summoned you out of the normal affairs of life and made you His own. You no more belong to yourself, you no more belong to your friends or family, you belong to God. Because you belong to him, you are His special interest. You are part of His master plan; you are involved in His global strategy. You are no longer plotting life on your own or running your own course, you have now been set apart to run His course. He is saying to you, 'I have my plans, I have my intentions, my programme for this world and while you are here, I summon you to be part of this programme. Don't ask what will I wear or eat, I will supply all. Before the creation of the world, you were foreknown and I predestined you the way I predestined Jesus.' When Jesus came he did not ask what will I eat,

He simply said,

> "Lo, I come (in the volume of the Book it is written of me) to do Your will, O God" (Hebrews 10:7 MKJV).

When it comes to God, you must understand that the way He deals with his sons and daughters is not the same way he deals with the world. If you look through history, you will find out that there is a particular thing about the way God leads and directs his people and it may seem to us that He somehow delays. It is an apparent delay, somehow we feel that God slows down when it comes to his own. For instance, God told Abraham that He will make him a great nation and he is going to be called the father of all nations. From the time God gave him this promise to the fulfillment of the promise, was twenty five years. Abraham was quite old and the wife has passed menopause before the performance of the promise.

When Samuel anointed David as the King of Israel, he was yet under 21 years, but it took several years of contention and fighting before David got to the throne. The scripture tells us about Jesus Christ, the Lamb that was slain from the inception of the world yet it took nothing less than five to six thousand years before the manifestation of Jesus on the surface of the earth. Why does God delay? Why does it seem that God allows his people to go through certain things? Does God do it purposely?

Peter in his 2nd letter wrote,

> "The Lord isn't really being slow about his promise to return as people think, no He is being patient for your sake" (2 Peter 3:9 NLT).

The Message Bible says,

> "God isn't late with his promise as some measure lateness. He is restraining himself on account of you..."

Who is an old man in the sight of God? Who has reached menopause that He cannot revitalize? Who has passed the prime of age that He cannot restore? **Psalms 90:4** says,

> "For a thousand years in your sight are as yesterday when it is past, and as a watch in the night."

WHEN THERE SEEMS TO BE A DELAY

While you are thinking of a thousand years, God is thinking of one day. To you there is a delay but before God, He is keeping to His promise, he is keeping to His plan. Sometimes I see our lives as an hourglass. As the sand drops from the upper to the lower part of the glass I can't help but wonder how long it will take for that top glass to empty. Many of us measure our lives with that of others based on our chronological age. We expect God to attend to us based on a particular time limit. We see our friends who have gone far ahead of us and we grumble. But God is asking 'do you know whether this man will end his journey at forty years while I have prepared you for one hundred years? Since I have prepared you for hundred years, why the hurry?

God understands the chronology of our life time, He has the time table. Don't bother about what you shall eat, only ensure that your life is in synchrony with the master plan of God for you. You see it as a delay because you are looking at someone else. Don't be worried, God is in the plan. When you think that there is a delay, it is good for you to be very careful because God has his plans and his plan is different from that of the world.

Don't take laws into your hands

I have seen several people take hasty steps when they feel there is a delay in their lives. If God would not do it on time, I will find a way around it. They take laws into their hands. One of the greatest tragedies of haste, found in the Bible, happened in the life of Saul. **1 Samuel 13:8-14** records:

> "Then he waited seven days, according to the time set by Samuel. But Samuel did not come to Gilgal; and the people were scattered from him. So Saul said, "Bring a burnt offering and peace offerings here to me." And he offered the burnt offering. Now it happened, as soon as he had finished presenting the burnt offering, that Samuel came; and Saul went out to meet him, that he might greet him. And Samuel said, "What have you done?" And Saul said, "When I saw that the people were scattered from me, and that you did not come within the days appointed, and that the Philistines gathered together at Michmash, then I said, 'The Philistines will now come down on me at Gilgal, and I have not made supplication to the LORD.' Therefore I felt compelled, and offered a burnt offering." And Samuel said to Saul, "You have

done foolishly. You have not kept the commandment of the LORD your God, which He commanded you. For now the LORD would have established your kingdom over Israel forever. But now your kingdom shall not continue. The LORD has sought for Himself a man after His own heart, and the LORD has commanded him to be commander over His people, because you have not kept what the LORD commanded you."

Saul took the laws into his hands and made a sacrifice he was not eligible to do and just as he was finishing the sacrifice, Samuel appeared. You may have set goals that never got achieved. However, do not be tempted to make it happen by forcing or manipulating things. Do not perform the sacrifice, like Saul. It happened in the life of Abraham. When the promised child was not forthcoming, Abraham and his wife, Sarah, decided to help God out of the predicament. The final consequence - they gave birth to the child that has become the thorn in the flesh of the nations of the world. That act of cooperating in haste never created harmony in the house of Abraham because he took the laws into his hands.

Don't develop a twisted mind-set

I have observed certain people, who having trusted God for success did not attain it, suddenly develop a philosophy of antagonism against everybody that is prosperous. Somehow their theology begins to change; they begin to react to people and situations. They begin to say evil things about those who have attained; their philosophy becomes twisted.

I think the period of delay is a time for you to check yourself, to ask, 'am I reacting because of my present condition or am I being objective about the facts before me? God does not expect us to begin to react and develop a twisted mentality, He expects better from us. This mind-set will make you a pessimistic and negative person and before you know you begin to judge the world through a narrow lens and see people through a distorted perspective.

Don't tune off

Many people lose the zest for life when they experience delays in their lives. They withdraw into themselves, would not associate with people and would seclude themselves. They see life as being very unfair; they feel

God is against them and they become depressed. There is nobody so easy to destroy by the devil as a person who has no friend. God created us to associate with one another and in this association lie our sanity. John Donne wrote: *"No man is an island, entire of itself; every man is a piece of the continent, a part of the main..."*

We must never cut off from the vast supply and numerous riches contained within the walls of friendship and companionship. Kaccipettu Nannakaiyar, an Indian poet who lived in the 3rd century wrote, *"I grow lean in loneliness, like a water lily gnawed by a beetle."* When we withdraw from people, we eventually lose out. We must never allow the challenges of life or the disappointment of existence close up the well of bubbling joy inside us. God has given us every good and sweet thing to enjoy. Though all things may not fall in place at once, we must learn to appreciate the gradual build-up of moments into what is called life.

Much more than tuning off, don't let something inside you die. Perhaps you have done an examination and failed several times, and then you begin to feel maybe there is something wrong with your intellect. Or you have spent a lot of time doing a particular work and encouragement is

> Greatness is maintaining optimism in desperate situations.

not coming from anywhere; nobody is impressed by your efforts, and somehow you begin to feel a sense of defeat. You feel you can no longer make it, you develop low self image, and when next you want to do the task, you go with the idea that you will not make it. Don't lose your enthusiasm; don't lose hope.

Periods of delay may be times when God wants to make your hard heart tender or toughen your feeble mind. Delay is a great period for self-discovery, self-development and growth in the vital areas of life. Don't fall into despair, use it as an opportunity to work on yourself. Greatness is maintaining optimism in desperate situations. No matter how desperate or tough your situation is, you must maintain your optimism. Give yourself the psychological pep talk you need. God has not yet finished with you, so do not lose the thrills of life.

Don't concentrate on the problems

Many people never rise above their circumstances because they focus on the problems rather than seek the solutions. This is exactly what Abraham did not do. Abraham did not focus on the deadness of Sarah's womb, he did not focus on her incapacity to bring forth a child. Rather he chose to focus on the promises of God. The Message Bible reports:

> **"Abraham didn't focus on his own impotence and say, "It's hopeless. This hundred-year-old body could never father a child." Nor did he survey Sarah's decades of infertility and give up. He didn't tiptoe around God's promise asking cautiously skeptical questions. He plunged into the promise and came up strong, ready for God, sure that God would make good on what he had said"** (Romans 4:19-21).

I don't know what you are focusing upon. Are you focusing on the fact that you have been praying for healing but your body remains the same? Are you focusing on the fact that you have been asking God for financial stability but it's not forthcoming? Stop focusing on the deadness of your Sarah's womb; stop focusing on the deadness of your Abraham's body, focus on the promises of God. When you focus on the promises of God, you will invariably wean yourself of the thinking of men, you'll realize that He has certain things in store for you.

Our lives come in various packages and no one can tell what is in the package of God for your life. Stop focusing on what has apparently been lost. I have counseled people who have told me that they wished they were not born. That life would have been better if they were not born. However, I believe when God wanted to bring you to this earth, he had certain things in mind. Don't focus on apparent failures. If you realize that the past is just a passing phase and the future holds great things for you, you can go through life walking tall. God plans for eternity while man settles for a time. God waits for the long haul while man looks for today's satisfaction. God gives blessings that have foundation, that will last a long time while men look for immediate results.

God has time in His hands

If you see what looks like an apparent delay, know that God has time in his hands. God has a particular time for everyone. **Galatians 6:9** says,

"So let's not allow ourselves to get fatigued doing good. At the right time we will harvest a

good crop if we don't give up, or quit" (MSG).

New Living Translation puts it this way:

"So don't get tired of doing what is good, don't get discouraged and give up; for we will reap a harvest of blessing at the appropriate time."

I don't know what the appropriate time is. However, if you look at the testimony of God down through the ages, you will discover God can be trusted to be faithful. I don't know what your period of waiting looks like. It may be a period of testing your faith. It may be a period of training you for godliness. It may be a period that God takes you through the school of humility so that you can be blessed. But I want to encourage you to persist. Do not be weary in well doing. Don't worry about the situation. Don't get anxious about the problems.

I want you to keep your anticipation high, keep your vision focused and believe that the dream God has given you is going to be achieved. Don't lose your dream, don't lose sight of the promise. Keep your enthusiasm alive. Remember, God specializes in making the small great, the insignificant important and the barren fruitful. Paul commented:

> "But God hath chosen the foolish things of the world to confound the wise; and God hath chosen the weak things of the world to confound the things which are mighty" (1 Corinthians 1:27)

No individual can stand the immense power of the living God. Apostle Paul said,

> "For a great door and effectual is opened unto me, and there are many adversaries" (1 Corinthians 16:9 KJV).

The presence of adversaries is not a call to give up - it is a call to press on. The truth is when we suffer long in our mission; we eventually reap a great reward. I found out that in the journey of life, people like to jump into any vehicle they think is prosperous. They start the journey thinking all will run smoothly and when it does not, they try to jump out. Many people have abandoned the course that God has given them, apparently because they were not making progress as they should. When things get tough, that is not the time to give up; rather it is the time for you to hold on. The Hebrew writer encouraged:

"Cast not away therefore your confidence, which hath great recompence of reward. For ye have need of patience, that, after ye have done the will of God, ye might receive the promise. For yet a little while, and he that shall come will come, and will not tarry. Now the just shall live by faith: but if any man draws back, my soul shall have no pleasure in him" (Hebrews 10:35-38 KJV).

Friend, can you stick with God? Can you persist with your vision? Can you persevere in the things God has promised you? I have discovered that men do not give us a chance; they focus on the flaws in our lives. But flaws or no flaws, mistakes or no mistakes, there is a divine plan. When God fulfills His dreams and plans, you will know that even in your mistakes, there is a pattern and in your failures, there is a divine focus.

Romans 8:28 says,

> "And we know that all things work together for good to them that love God, to them who are the called according to his purpose" (KJV).

God has a plan and as you keep waiting on him, never

give up. One of my best scripture verses is **Habakkuk 2:3**,

> "For the vision is yet for an appointed time, but at the end it shall speak, and not lie: though it tarry, wait for it; because it will surely come, it will not tarry."

There is an appointed time for every ministry, there is an appointed time for every calling; there is an appointed time for every establishment. We are not in anybody's race. Someone may enter into the Guinness Book of record for becoming a millionaire at the age of 16 - that is his race. The burden of managing one million at the age of 16 is much more than having a million at the age of thirty; but it is his race. Your vision is for an appointed time; don't spend time concentrating on your neighbour's garden, tend your own. Keep on trying in trying times and keep on sowing in adverse weather. One day your efforts will bear fruits. *It shall speak, and not lie: though it tarry, wait for it; because it will surely come.* James wrote,

> "Behold, we count them happy which endure. Ye have heard of the patience of Job, and have seen

> the end of the Lord; that the Lord is very pitiful, and of tender mercy" (James 5:11 KJV).

The Greek word for the 'end of the Lord' is not death; it is the goal of God. It is the plan of the Lord, the finishing point of God. It is the completion of God's purpose for your life; it is the conclusion of God. It is the summary of God, the quest of God and the intention of God. The Lord is very pitiful and of tender mercy. God knows how you feel; and He feels what you feel. He is touched with the feeling of your infirmities.

The energy required to wait a little longer is just what you need to arrive at the destination.

> "For we have not an high priest which cannot be touched with the feeling of our infirmities; but was in all points tempted like as we are, yet without sin" (Hebrews 4:15 KJV).

Regardless of what is going on, God has the conclusion. He has the goal, not the third chapter but the whole book. I believe that at the end of life, you can say like Jeremiah,

> "This I recall to my mind, therefore have I hope. It is of the LORD'S mercies that we are not consumed, because his compassions fail not.

They are new every morning: great is thy faithfulness." (Lamentations 3:21-23)

Do you want to give up now? Just wait a little while. The energy required to wait a little longer is just what you need to arrive at the destination.

CHAPTER NINE

HOW GREAT MEN HANDLED THEIR WORRY

> There are two days in the week,
> about which and upon which I never worry.
> Two carefree days,
> kept sacredly free from fear and apprehension.
> One of these days is Yesterday.
> And the other day I do not worry about is
> Tomorrow.
> **Robert Jones Burdette**

In life, we daily have to make choices - to act and bring about a change in our lives or to allow life act on us by surrendering our will to it, to overcome the worries that plagues us and live a triumphant life or be daily saddled and defeated by our greatest fears; to subject our thoughts and imagination to the positive influence of the

Word of God or to be carried along on the tide of negativity and despair. Every day presents you with a choice and what you choose will determine where you end.

Through the years, men have faced the challenge to overcome the habit of worry. They have had to face situations that seemed impossible to surmount, they have had to choose between living as a victim or as a victor. And these choices have separated the remembered from the forgotten. Written in this chapter are insights into the lives of people who have lived before us or are still living, and how they handled their worries. Some have probably faced what we are facing now but they found a way of rising above their worries and doing the task that has been committed to them. They are great men, both in the biblical and contemporary times, who chose to ignore the problems and pursue the goal.

MARTIN LUTHER

Martin Luther was a great man of God. He was the father of Protestantism. He wrote this on how he coped with worry:

'When I am assailed with heavy tribulations, I rush out among my pigs rather that remain alone by myself. The human heart is like a millstone in a mill; when you put wheat under it, it turns and grinds and bruises the wheat to flour; if you put no wheat, it still grinds on but then, it is itself it grinds and wears away. So the human heart, unless it be occupied with some employment leaves space for the devil, who wriggles himself in and brings with him a whole host of evil thoughts, temptations and tribulations which grind out the heart.'

What is Martin Luther advocating as a cure for worry? If all the thoughts that go through our minds are given the chance of the day, they will ruin our lives and never allow us to get to the destination. When plagued with worries, give your heart something to do. Swing into action and subdue the intruders.

THE GRAHAM FAMILY - RUTH BELL GRAHAM

Ruth Bell Graham is the wife of the world-renowned evangelist, Billy Graham. When one of her sons was living a wild and dangerous life, she found herself torn apart by worry. One night while traveling overseas she suddenly awoke. A current of fear surged through her like an electric shock. She lay in bed and tried to pray, but she suffered from galloping anxiety, one fear piling upon another. She looked at the clock and it was around three o'clock.

She was exhausted, yet she knew she would be unable to go back to sleep. Suddenly, the Lord seemed to say to her, 'Quit studying the problems and start trusting the promises.' She turned on the light, got out her Bible and the first verses that came to her were **Philippians 4: 6-7**, *"Do not be anxious about anything but in everything by prayer and petition with thanksgiving, present your requests to God. And the peace of God which transcends all understanding will guard your hearts and your minds in Christ Jesus."* As she read those words, she suddenly realized that the missing ingredient in her prayers had been thanksgiving. *"...In everything by prayer and petition, with thanksgiving, present your requests to God."*

> Quit studying the problems and start trusting the promises.

She put down her Bible and spent time worshipping God

for who and what He is. She later wrote, "I began to thank God for giving me this one I loved so dearly in the first place. I even thanked him for the difficult spots, which had taught me so much. And you know what happened? It was as if someone turned on the light in my mind and heart and the little fears and worries that had been nibbling away in the darkness like mice and cockroaches hurriedly scuttled for cover. That was when I learned that worship and worry cannot live in the same heart. They are mutually exclusive."

* * *

When worry overwhelms you, stop studying the problems and start reminding yourself of the promises. The challenges of life must never be permitted to cloud our minds or veil our faces from the plan and purpose of God. Remember the promises and give thanks.

BILLY GRAHAM

Billy Graham in his autobiography 'Just as I am' described these same difficult years when their sons were away from the Lord:

'Ruth and I found that for us, worrying and praying were mutually exclusive. We trusted the Lord to bring the children through somehow in His own way in due time. On day-to-day basis, however, we muddled through. But God was faithful. Today, each of them is filled with faith and fervor for the Lord's service.'

* * *

When the situation is difficult and the mountains seem immovable, we can always talk to our Father in heaven about it. He holds the master plan and has the ability to handle all our problems. We can learn to trust God to bring us out of the dark tunnels of life in the bright light of His glory. Why worry when you can pray.

ROBERT H. SCHULLER

Dr. Robert Schuller is the pastor of the world famous Crystal Cathedral at Garden Grove in California. He is an inspirational speaker who has a television ministry in the United States of America. In his book, *'Tough times never last but tough people do,'* he related his experience about worry and fear when his daughter Carol Schuller got involved in a motorcycle accident and was seriously injured:

"Flying back on the lonely torturing trip from Korea to America, after Carol's motorcycle accident, I was overwhelmed with grief and worry. I wept. I prayed. Out of this time of deep prayer, a sentence, as clear as if it were sky written against the clouds passed through my mind: 'Play it down and pray it up.' I took that as a direct message from God. To me it meant this: 'Don't exaggerate the problem. You are playing it up too much. She did not lose both legs. She has had no head injury. She suffered no brain damage. No vital organs are permanently impaired. She is not in a life-threatening situation. You are totally exaggerating the impact of the accident. Play it down. Then pray it up. Give it to God and give God a chance to show how the scars can be turned into stars. Did God intervene? Yes, he did!"

> Play it down and pray it up.

When we arrived from Korea to Carol's bedside in Sioux City, Iowa, I was shocked. She lay in bed in intensive care. Her body was bruised, broken and disfigured. But her spirits were whole and healthy. On the long trip back, I had searched for my opening line. What would my first words to her be? She solved the problem by speaking first: "I know why it happened, Dad. God wants to use me to help others who have been hurt."

It was this spirit, this positive attitude that carried her through seven months of hospitalisation and intravenous feedings. This positive attitude gave her the courage to fight a raging infection that threatened her limb and her life. It was that same positive attitude that helped Carol make transition from hospital patient to a handicapped member of a family and school. It helped her feel normal and whole again!"

*   *   *

Within every person is the capacity to rise above his circumstances and find a solution to his problem. It might not be as bad as you think. Play it down and pray it up. Change to a positive mental attitude and turn your bruises to blessings.

CHARLES ALLEN

In one of his books, Methodist Pastor Charles Allen narrated his visit to a particular city. Being met at the plane, he was told, "We don't have time to wait for your baggage. Someone else will get it. You are to speak at a club in twenty minutes." Rushing from the airport, Allen learned he was to speak each morning on television at nine, at church at ten, and somewhere else each evening. He was also to address three civic clubs, two high schools and one women's meeting. In all, he had nineteen speaking arrangements in four days plus a series of personal interviews. By Wednesday night, Allen found himself wound so tightly he scarcely slept a wink. The worries and pressures got to him.

The next day he rebelled. After the morning engagements, he said, 'I told the pastor I would be gone for the remainder of the day. I started walking slowly down the street, going no place in particular and in no hurry to get there. A number of people spoke to me and stopped and talked awhile. It reminded me of living in a little town where you can enjoy visiting up and down Main Street. I walked on past the city limits until I came to a big bridge on the river. I found a comfortable place to sit down and I sat there for two hours watching the river.

From the bridge I could see the point where two rivers flowed together. One of the rivers was almost clear, the other extremely muddy. For a short distance, after they came together you could distinguish the water of each, but a little further on, the clear water took on the brownish colour of the other. I thought about how we let evil thoughts come into our minds and how the evil soon colours all our living. I made some mental notes for a sermon about that. At the end of the bridge was a tiny hamburger place. I had one with onion; in fact, I asked for an extra onion. It tasted real good. I didn't care whether or not it left an odour on my breath. I had been so pious all that week that I was in the mood to do something daring. I walked along the street until I came to a cemetery... and spent an hour walking among the graves. During that hour I was the only person there. I thought about how quickly someone is forgotten and how others take our places. It is not so important that we carry the world on our shoulders as we sometimes think.

I got back to the hotel for dinner before the preaching service that night. I felt rested and relaxed. When I got back to my room after service, I went to bed. I picked up my Bible from the table and opened it to the thirty seventh Psalm. It was written for people who get disturbed and overly wrought up. The thirty seventh Psalm is gentle and tender; like a sweet kindly mother putting her hand upon the brow of a restless child. The

Psalm begins, "Fret not thyself..." It goes on to say, "Delight thyself also in the Lord, and He shall give thee the desire of thy heart." Further on we read, "Rest in the Lord, and wait patiently for him..." All the way through, the Psalm leads one to a calm and triumphant faith. That night I slept easily and the next day I felt rested and strong.

* * *

We weren't made for a non-stop twenty-four hour frantic pace. We need to take time for ourselves, time to relax, time to walk by the still waters, time waiting before the Lord, for there alone can we renew our strength and overcome worry. When the pressure gets high, get away.

DAVID

David was a beloved man of God. He was the youngest son of Jesse and Nahash, chosen of God to be king of Israel. Being a shepherd turned warrior, he encountered a lot of troubles before and after he became the king. After defeating Goliath, he faced serious opposition from Saul. Constant threats were made on his life and Saul made twenty-one attempts to kill him before his (Saul) death. Without any doubt, David was a man full of worry and fear for his life.

David's years in exile were spent in distress and despair. He longed for his home and desired in his heart to return to Jerusalem. In Psalm 42 he wrote.

> "My inner self thirsts for God for the living God. When shall I come and behold the face of God? My tears have been my food day and night, while men say to me all day long. Where is your God? ... Why are you cast down, my inner self? And why should you moan over me and be disquieted within me?" (Psalm 42: 2-3, 5).

We see a distressing situation in the life of David which was documented in the first book of Samuel.

> "And it came to pass, when David and his men were come to Ziklag on the third day, that the Amalekites had invaded the south, and Ziklag and smitten Ziklag and burned it with fire. And had taken the women captives that were therein: they slew not any, either great or small but carried them away, and went on their way... then David and the people that were with him lifted up their voice and wept until they had no more power to weep. ... and David was greatly

distressed; for the people spake of stoning him because the soul of all the people was grieved, every man for his sons and for his daughters but David encouraged himself in the Lord his God" (I Samuel 30:1-2, 4, 6).

David had gone to the land of the Philistines for battle only to return home to discover that the Amalekites had smitten Ziklag and burned it down. At that moment, great sorrow and anxiety descended upon them all. David was greatly distressed because the grieved multitude thought of stoning him. But David encouraged himself in the Lord. This is an important lesson to us. When faced with difficult and disheartening situations, we should learn to encourage ourselves in the Lord.

One good thing that showed clearly in David's life was his ability to hand over all his problems to God. He was so much in tune with God that he talked to Him like a man would talk to his friend. Having recognized the supremacy of God and His loving-kindness at all times, David maximized on it throughout his life. This was reflected in **Psalm 42:5** when he said,

"...Hope in God and wait expectantly for Him, for I shall yet praise Him, my help and my God.

> O my God, my life is cast down upon me and I find the burden more than I can bear; therefore will I earnestly remember you from the land of the Jordan River and the summits of mount Hermon from the little mountain Mizar."

The depth of his depression could also be felt in Psalm 88 as he called on God:

> "O Lord the God who saves me day and night I cry out before you. May my prayer come before you, turn your ear to my cry. For my soul is full of trouble and my life draws near the grave."

David recognized his helplessness and turned to the Lord. He declared in **Psalm 46:1-2**,

> "God is our refuge and strength an ever-present help in trouble, Therefore we will not fear though the earth give way and the mountains fall into the heart of the sea."

What a marvellous way of declaring an unshakeable faith in God! David loved God and trusted Him and God acknowledged this by helping him to overcome his enemies and lifting him to the throne as king of Israel.

* * *

Do you trust God enough to hand over your worries to Him like David did? Can you boldly say that though the mountains fall into the sea you will neither fear nor worry? Worry is anti-faith; you either have faith or you worry. Acknowledge the sovereignty of God and cease to worry.

HEZEKIAH

Hezekiah was one of the kings of Judah. He trusted in the Lord, the God of Israel and there was no one like him among all the kings of Judah, either before him or after him (2 Kings 18:5). The Bible went further to say that *"He held fast to the Lord and did not cease to follow him; he kept the commands the Lord had given Moses"* (Verse 6).

But all these did not give him an automatic peaceful time while he reigned as king. He had many troubles and faced many challenges, which got him seriously worried. The king of Assyria, Sennacherib, has captured all the fortified cities of Judah and Hezekiah was afraid. It was this fear and worry that drove him to give his word to the king of Assyria in **2 Kings 18:14**,

> "...I have done wrong. Withdraw from me and I will pay whatever you demand of me..."

He signed a treaty he could not sustain; his worries drove him to take a drastic step, which later had a rebound effect. It led to the king of Assyria asking for more than he could afford and Hezekiah had to strip off the gold with which he had covered the doors of the temple of the Lord. He gave what belonged to God out to an ordinary man. Why? He was fearful and worried. However, Sennacherib was not satisfied. He requested for more and when the people of Judah did not respond, he wrote a letter to them foretelling their destruction. This was when Hezekiah realised that he could no longer handle it alone.

2 Kings 19:14 records:

> "Hezekiah received the letter from the messengers and read it. Then he went up to the temple of the Lord and spread it out before the Lord. And Hezekiah prayed to the Lord."

It came to a time in King Hezekiah's life when it dawned on him that the solution to the problem lies with God. Rather than fret or worry over it, he took the letter down to the temple and spread it out before God. He chose to lay his burdens and anxieties at the feet of the Lord. And God took it up! God spoke concerning the king of Assyria,

> "He will not enter this city or shoot an arrow here; He will not come before it with shield or build a siege camp against it. By the way that he came he will return; he will not enter his city. I will defend this city and save it for my sake and for the sake of David my servant. That night the angel of the Lord went out and put to death a hundred and eighty-five thousand men in the Assyrian camp" (2 Kings 19:32-35).

That was a manifestation of God's power. Without lifting a hand, God won the battle for Hezekiah.

* * *

God is able to deal with all our troubles if we cast them upon Him. Like David said, He is a present help in time of trouble. Cast all your anxieties on Him.

JOSEPH

Joseph was a man who exemplified the principle of

maximizing the present circumstance on the way to greatness. He was loved by his father. However, the favouritism was so evident that his brothers grew jealous and sold him into slavery. His dreams were shattered. A man who formerly enjoyed the loving attention of his father became a slave attending to the needs of other people; a servant who had no choice or will of his own. But there was something peculiar about Joseph; he chose to make the best of the way things turned out. He chose a positive reaction to the circumstances. Rather than worry about how life had turned, he decided to put in exemplary service in Potiphar's house. With the grace of God upon him and as a result of his remarkable accomplishments, Potiphar made him overseer over his estate (Genesis 39:4).

However, his troubles and miseries were not yet over. He was unfairly accused of attempted rape and was jailed without a court hearing. Surprisingly, instead of giving up all hope and sinking into despair, Joseph adapted quickly to life in prison. God was with him and he soon became a prisoner cum warder; he was put in charge of fellow prisoners. However, Joseph did not just stop at accepting his condition, he saw an opportunity and he acted upon it. God had given him the gift of interpretation of dreams and he was able to interpret the dreams of the King's Cupbearer and Baker. The interpretation favoured the cupbearer but it did not favour the Baker. In **Genesis 40:41** after interpreting the dream of the cupbearer Joseph said,

> "But when all goes well with you remember me and show me kindness; mention me to Pharaoh and get me out of this prison."

He saw an opportunity and maximized it. Though the cupbearer forgot him, eventually a situation arose which caused him to be remembered. That was the breakthrough needed for his elevation- and a prisoner became the prime minister.

* * *

May be your condition is as bad as Joseph's. Maybe life is passing you by and you are stuck in the slow lane. You need to emulate Joseph and stick it out. Do your best where you are and stop worrying. Accept what you cannot change and maximize your opportunities.

JESUS CHRIST

Our Lord Jesus Christ was not exempted from worry and depression and He is our model of absolute control of it. He had fulfilled his teaching ministry and his life on earth was gradually coming to a close. Knowing the manner in which He would die, He started dreading it. That was what led him to the garden of Gethsemane. **Mark 14:33-36** says:

> "He took Peter, James and John along with him and he began to be deeply distressed and troubled. "My soul is overwhelmed with sorrow to the point of death," he said to them. "Stay here and keep watch". Going a little further, he fell to the ground and prayed that if possible the hour might pass from him. "Abba, Father," he said, 'if it is possible, may this cup be taken from me. Yet not as I will but as you will."

'If it is possible'- that statement marked the depth of Jesus' depression and distress. He wanted the hour to pass but his next statement portrayed his total submission to the will of God. Jesus was a man given to prayer. He knew the efficacy and usefulness of prayer in every situation and he took solace in praying when trouble drew near.

Yet in prayer he accepted whatever God has planned concerning him. He knew the importance of his death in the redemption of the world and accepted his condition and position as the saviour of men.

'Not as I will but as You will' is a statement that showed the depth of Jesus' absolute belief and trust in the power of God. He gave complete control to Him. He knew he couldn't change the situation. It had been destined from the beginning of the world. It was the only means to save the world. Jesus cooperated with the inevitable and received strength in prayer. After praying, the angels ministered to him and he was ready to face the cross. **Mark 14:42** says,

"**Rise! Let us go! Here comes my betrayer!**"

He was ready to meet his betrayer. Confidence and strength had suddenly flooded him. That is what we get when we offload our hearts to God in prayer. We will feel relieved and strong enough to face the unavoidable.

* * *

Prayer is communion with a caring God; it gives us the power over stressful conditions and renews our strength and ability to face life's challenges. Accept the inevitable and pray for strength to overcome it.

CHAPTER TEN

YOU MUST QUIT WORRYING NOW

> What's the use of worrying?
> It never was worthwhile
> So pack up your troubles in your old kit-bag,
> And smile, smile, smile.
> **George Asaf**

One important tool of survival God gave us as humans is our will power. The prerogative of the will gives you the authority to choose and to act. It gives you the power of attorney over your actions and your response to the circumstances that you face every day.

The strength of your will, will determine whether you will succumb to the forces of despair or break the chains of pessimism. It determines whether you will submit to the caprices of worry and depression or rise against the tide of self-pity to reach out to a world that beckons on your destiny. A time must come in the life of a man when he must begin to spin the wheel of change, not just in his life but in the world around him. I believe it is time to rise beyond the worries that plague us and begin to pursue our mission for life.

Everyone you come across has a problem. The great people you read about have diverse problems. Robert Schuller wrote, *"Nobody is free from problems. A problem free life is an illusion- a mirage in the desert. It is a dangerously deceptive perception, which can mislead, blind and distract."* What determines greatness is your ability not to build a tent round your problem. Rather extend a helping hand to the next person. Worry can never solve any problem. It is going to too much trouble for very little. The secret of happiness in life lies in overcoming our fears and helping someone else do the same.

Psalm 37:8 says,

"Stop your anger! Turn off your wrath. Don't fret and worry it only leads to harm.' (TLB)

George Macdonald wrote, "No man ever sank under the burden of the day. It is when tomorrow's burden is added to the burden of today that the weight is more than a man can bear. Never load yourself so. If you find yourself so loaded, at least remember this: it is your own doing, not God's. He begs you to leave the future to him and mind the present." Know your load limit. God is the pump and you are the pipe. Worry must never be your way of life! You can win over the situation if you can make a strong decision and stand by it. Taking the first step towards gaining your freedom might be difficult. But once you take that bold step, you are on your way to victory.

There are two situations in which you must never worry- when you can solve the problem and when you cannot. Go about your business keeping your mind focused. Throw worry behind you and do the job at hand. If you do the best and the most you can today, tomorrow will take care of itself. Stop worrying before it stops you; you can be the next great man the world wants to know his secret!

EPILOGUE

In the bid to overcome life's pressures and anxieties, one thing is paramount a relationship with God. He alone can sustain and strengthen us when all hope is lost. His shoulders can bear us through the troubles and storms of life. Why not give God a chance in your life today? Can you please join me in this prayer:

> **Dear Lord, I commit my life to you. I am sorry for how I have lived a life of continuous anxiety and worry, rebelling against your word and running my life my way. I confess my sins of unbelief and lack of trust and receive you into my life; I ask that Jesus will come into my heart. I hand over my worries to you; I choose to cast my cares on you and trust you with my life. Help me to surmount the pressures of life and live a victorious life in Jesus. I dedicate my life to you,**

O Lord. All this I pray in the name of your Son Jesus Christ, Amen.

Now that you have read this book and have begun a fresh relationship with Christ, I believe you are set for a brand new life in Christ Jesus. You can share your experience with me. I would like to hear from you.

> **Please write:**
> Rev. Prof. G. E. Erhabor P.
> O. Box 1154, Ile-Ife
> gregerhabor7@yahoo.com
> www.spokesmancom.org

THE POWER OF JOY

Joy is not a product of chance but an expression of the Spirit of God in us. You can be joyful always regardless of the circumstances.

This book will teach you how to stay joyful and win over the spirit of depression and sadness.

SEIZE YOUR DAY; CONTROL YOUR DESTINY

The best way to invent the future is to purposefully channel everyday. When we make the best of today, we make the best of life.

This book will teach you how to harness and effectively utilize the potentials inherent in your mornings.

REVISED EDITION
PRINCIPLES OF ACADEMIC EXCELLENCE
---※---

This book is a must-read for those who desire to excel academically and maintain their passion for God. It is the synthesis of over three decades of experience in active Christian leadership and constant academic pursuit. The book gives you practical steps on how you can be academically smart and spiritually sound. It is a book that will put your doubts to rest.

REVISED EDITION
THE SEVEN MOST EFFECTIVE AFFIRMATIONS TOWARDS ACHIEVING YOUR GOALS

———❈———

Biblically, affirmations are proclamations of faith. They are declarations that determine our destiny and pilot our lives. The Seven Affirmations are simple statements that would help us live a productive life and fulfill our purpose.

It is handy for all occasions.

REVISED EDITION

YOUR TIME IN YOUR HANDS

The quality of our lives will be largely determined by how we manage our time.

Greatness comes as a result of effective planning, diligent work and most especially, brilliancy in managing time.

This is a must-read for everyone who wants to maximize every moment and leave an indelible mark for generations to come.

FROM WORRY TO WELL-BEING

THE MAKING OF A
GREAT PASTOR

Great pastors are those who leave a long-lasting legacy behind. They do not only build institutions, they build men. They have an excellent spirit. To them being called to serve, is a privilege, not a right. These pastors do not emphasize what men owe them but see themselves as being called to serve.

Looking for a book that will ignite your passion for ministry and give you added impetus to serve God and build men in your local church? This is the book for you. It is filled with practical principles on how you can build your life, build men under your care and leave a long-lasting legacy behind.

OTHER BOOKS BY THE AUTHOR

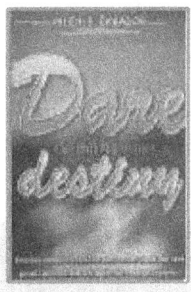

DARE TO FULFILL YOUR DESTINY

Everyone who reads this book, regardless of his present status, age or calling can discover in it practical steps on how to maximize his life and turn momentary set backs into monumental opportunities.

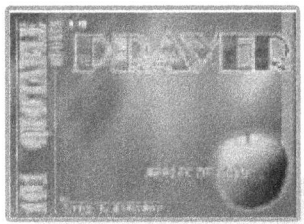

101 QUOTABLE QUOTES ON PRAYER- APPLES OF GOLD

Effective prayer depends on a good understanding of the subject. This book serves as a quick resource material on the subject of prayer.

COMMITMENT: THE HALLMARK OF GREATNESS

This book addresses the question: 'What will I do to change my generation? And not 'What can I get from my generation? It will teach you how to move from mere interest to commitment to a noble cause, mission or institution. It will teach you how you can leave your footprints on the sands of time and move your generation forward towards positive and long-lasting achievement.

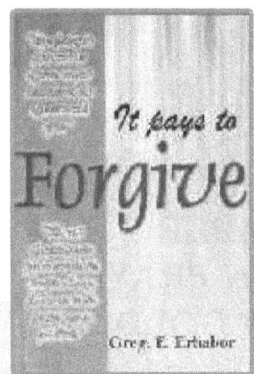

IT PAYS TO FORGIVE

An ounce of forgiveness is worth several pounds of medicine. Forgiveness is the greatest therapeutic agent to keep your head, heart and stomach from the physician's medication and the surgeon's scalpel. It really pays to forgive. This book will tell you how and why you must make forgiveness a lifestyle and begin to swim in the ocean of inner serenity. It is a book that will surely turn your destiny around.

GOD-CENTERED PROSPERITY

Prosperity is not the right of an exclusive club. God designed that we all prosper in all we do. Biblical prosperity comes when we come to terms with the principles laid down by God in His word. This book will help you attain to true prosperity without compromising your principles. You too can be prosperous and holy.

MAKING YOUR LIFE COUNT

We all have the ability to impact our generation and make our lives count. This book will help you rise above the drudgery of everyday living and put a touch of nobility in all you do.

THE TEST, TRAVAILS AND TRIUMPH OF LEADERSHIP

This contemporary insight into the life of Gideon and his men will teach you the principles of becoming the great leader you desire to be. It will also help you develop the abilities required to surmount obstacles and establish God's purpose in your life and the lives of those God has called you to lead.
It is a book for all leaders in all walks of life, both in spiritual and secular callings. You can be the Gideon of today to give the inspired leadership to your generation.

SEEDS OF EXCELLENCE

Excellence is an ever increasing quest! It can be practised by everybody. This book will inspire you to aspire to something beyond the ordinary. It will lift you up from the quick sand of mediocrity to the solid rock of excellence and greatness.

www.ingramcontent.com/pod-product-compliance
Lightning Source LLC
Chambersburg PA
CBHW071451040426
42444CB00008B/1293